Piercing the Eggshell

The Hubers
and their
Astrological Psychology

Edited and researched by
Barry & Joyce Hopewell

HopeWell
Knutsford, England

First published in English in 2020 by HopeWell

HopeWell,
130 Grove Park, Knutsford
Cheshire WA16 8QD, U.K.

Jacket: design by Barry Hopewell
using image adapted from Bruno Huber's Amphora diagram

Horoscopes: Huber-Method
(drawn up with MegaStar software)

ISBN 978-0-9956736-5-6

Louise & Bruno Huber

*"we feel close to a 'new science of man,'
wherein modern psychological perception and
ancient astrological wisdom are blended"*

from the introduction to *Man and His World*, 1975

*"Uranus is an instrument we use
to pierce through the eggshell towards spirituality"*

Froebel College, 1988

About the Editors

Barry Hopewell has been chief editor of the publisher HopeWell since its founding in 2003, publisher of the Huber books in English. Also a trustee of the Astrological Psychology Association since 2003 and has fulfilled various roles related to its publications.

After obtaining her Diploma in Astrological Psychology, Joyce Hopewell became Principal of the English Huber School in 1991. She continued to play a leading role as Principal, then Principal Emeritus, until the closure of the School's teaching programme at the end of 2019.

Acknowledgements

This book documents the achievements of two remarkable individuals, Bruno & Louise Huber. They inspired its coming into being.

Much of the content of this book has been taken from material that originally appeared in the German-language magazine *Astrolog*. We are indebted to Bruno & Louise Huber, and subsequently to Internationaler Fachverband für Astrologische Pychologie (IFAP), for permission to use material from that magazine. Similarly, there is input taken from the English-language magazine of Astrological Psychology Association (APA), *Conjunction*, for which we must thank its contributors and editors, notably Richard Llewellyn, Joyce Hopewell, Sara Inkster, Barry Hopewell, Caroline Adlestone.

This book would not have been possible in this form without the individual contributions and suggestions made by Richard Llewellyn, Sue Lewis and Sue Cameron (UK), Rosa Solé Gubianes and Lola Ferrer (Spain), Ana Quiroga (Chile), Angela Wilfart (France), Juan Saba (Argentina), Pam Tyler and Samantha Breno (USA), Michael Huber (via Samantha), Harald Zittlau, Wolfhard König and Elke Gut (Germany), and Bruno Landolt (Switzerland).

Special thanks are due to Sue Lewis for translating material from Spanish, for reviewing and proofing the draft, and for making valuable suggestions. Also to Harald Zittlau for helping to clarify the course of events leading to the establishment of IFAP.

In fact we are indebted to the whole astrological-psychological Huber/API family who have shared this challenging, fulfilling and enjoyable journey of exploration into ourselves and others. Only the tip of the iceberg is presented in this book.

Contents

Foreword

Before memories are lost in the mists of time, we wanted to tell the story of how a young Swiss/German couple came up with a revolution in astrology and psychology based on deep spiritual principles, yet very practical in its application. They aimed to create a 'new science of man', and a process to facilitate psychological and spiritual development using astrology.

As with all revolutionary movements, this one was not widely accepted and adopted at the time by either the astrological community or the many strands of modern psychology. Yet thousands of Europeans and seekers from all over the world were inspired to make this new 'astrological psychology' a part of their lives, and to use it in the helping of others towards their own growth process.

Our aim is to give a biographical and historical outline to help you the reader understand why this couple and their astrological psychology proved such an exciting venture.

Bruno and Louise Huber have since passed away, but their teaching lives on, now in numerous books and with practitioners in many parts of the German-, English-, and Spanish-speaking worlds. This is their story, and the story of those who came along for this particular great adventure towards a more rounded and holistic humanity.

Barry & Joyce Hopewell

November 2020

1. Introduction

Approach

We aim to tell the story of the lives and achievements of Bruno & Louise[1] Huber in the context of their times, and what they inspired in others.

Where possible we have used the words of Bruno & Louise themselves and the many like-minded members of what became the astrological-psychological 'Huber family' or 'API Family', who were inspired to help, learn about, research and use their system of astrological psychology. We believe that this will give you a better feel for the Hubers and their Method than would a more abstract third person narrative. To help the narrative flow, quoted text is fully indented with spacing between paragraphs, rather than using quotation marks or italicised text.

To read this book you do not need to know any astrology, nor have a deep knowledge of psychology. But for those who do, we relate the Hubers' lives to the astrological features in their own birth charts, highlighting key features of their approach to astrological chart interpretation. You can simply ignore such astrological asides, or try to make some sense of them. For the latter case, we have provided a simple outline of key features of the Huber Method on page 2 onward.

We present on page 4 their natal birth charts in the format developed by Bruno himself, these will be referred to along the way. If you pause briefly to look at the patterns of coloured lines in them, you will see that Bruno's chart appears dynamic and triangular, with what look like mountain peaks at the top of the chart. On the other hand, Louise's chart looks solid, square, stable and dependable. Even at this level we are starting to use the Hubers' approach to chart interpretation and have started to gain some understanding of the difference between their individual characters.

---

1 'Louise' is pronounced with the 'e' enunciated as in 'the' or the French 'le', so sounds much like 'Louisa'.

The Huber Method

This overview will enable you to better appreciate the Huber system.

Psychological-spiritual model

Underlying astrological psychology is a model of the human psyche that was developed by Italian psychologist Roberto Assagioli in his psychology of psychosynthesis. The Egg model of the personality takes into account the transpersonal or spiritual dimensions of experience[2].

In the centre of the Egg is the conscious personal self, surrounded by its field of conscious self awareness (the circle). Other parts of the Egg's interior represent various aspects of the unconscious. At the top is the Higher Self, the link with our divine or spiritual nature.

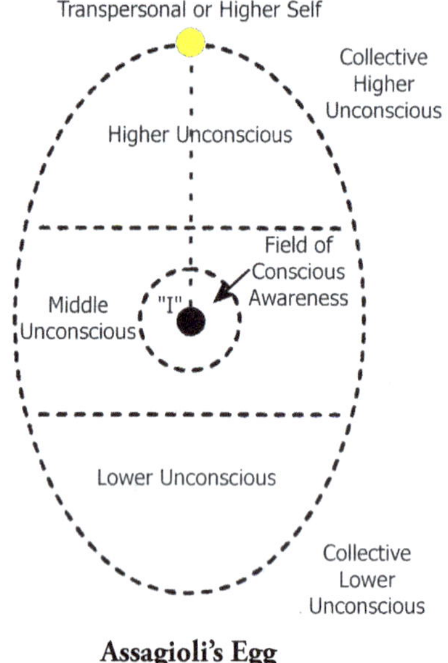

Assagioli's Egg

The aim of astrological psychology is twofold. Firstly, to help us become aware of those unconscious influences that are holding us back thus enabling us to grow a healthy ego, *within the egg*, and secondly, to help awaken our intuitive faculties to enable us to *pierce the eggshell* and break through to become our true spiritual selves.

---

2 Egg Model – see e.g. Will Parfitt, *Psychosynthesis: The Elements and Beyond*, PS Avalon, 2015.

Astrological charts

The coloured astrological chart format devised by Bruno Huber is unique to this system. You can refer to the charts of Bruno & Louise Huber on page 4 to familiarise yourself with these features.

The Five Levels

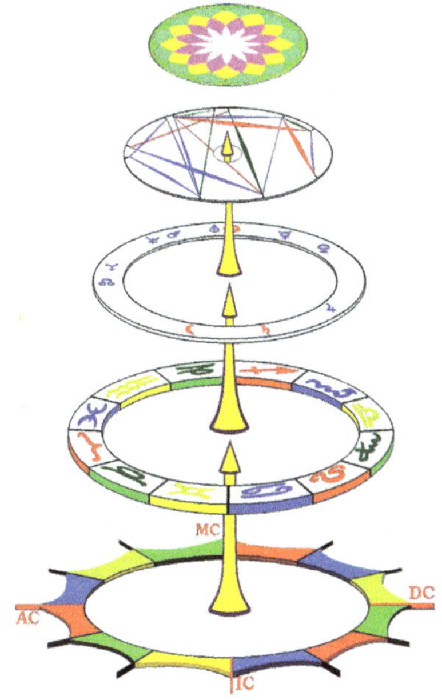

Centre circle, our inner essential being, doorway to universal energies

Aspects, and the pattern of lines, inner motivation

Planets, capabilities and tools of the personality

Signs, inherited traits and archetypal qualities

Houses, the environment, where and how we interact with the world

There are five distinct layers in a Huber chart[3].

The houses

- The 12 houses are divided into 4 quadrants by
  - The Ascendant rising on the Eastern horizon corresponding to the time of birth and the cusp of house 1 (AC);
  - The Imum Coeli in the Northern depths of unconscious roots, the cusp of house 4 (IC);
  - The Descendant on the Western horizon, the cusp of house 7 of partnership (DC);
  - The Medium Coeli, or Midheaven, the Southern angle at the top of the chart where an individual is most visible in the community, the cusp of house 10 (MC).

---

3 Graphic of five levels by Michael Huber.

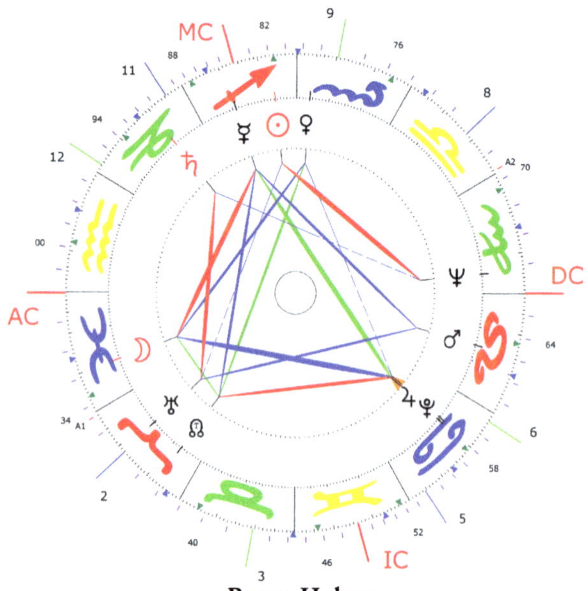

Bruno Huber
29/11/1930, 12:55, Zürich, Switzerland

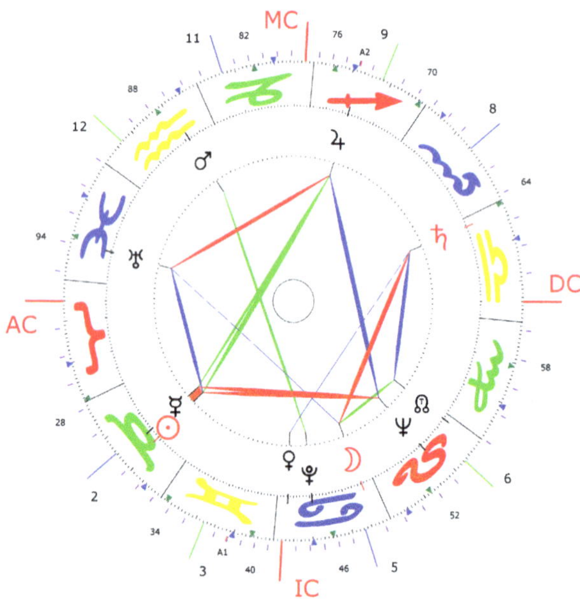

Louise Huber
10/05/1924, 03:15, Bamberg, Germany

- The houses are drawn using the Koch birthplace system, which divides each quadrant into three houses with cusps corresponding to divisions of time between dawn, midday, sunset and midnight. This is the only house system that the Hubers found to give reliable psychological correlations.
- There is a Dynamic Energy Curve in the chart, which results in special points in each house: Balance Point (BP) around a third of the way from the cusp (shown as small blue triangle on the outer circle of the chart), and Low Point (LP) around two thirds from the cusp (green triangle). Outgoing energy is high near cusp, balanced around BP, but low near LP, which is correspondingly close to the inner essence.

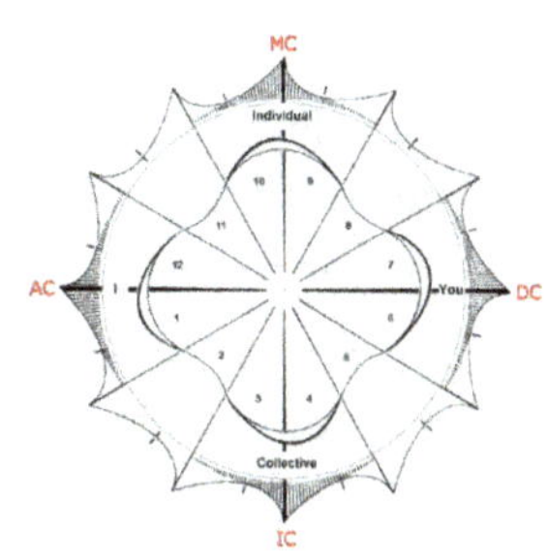

Dynamic Energy Curve

- Age Progression. The Age Point (AP) starts at birth at the AC and moves anticlockwise around the chart, 6 years per house. For the purposes of this book only, the position of the age point marker is highlighted in purple on some charts for easy identification. See for example the chart on page 12.

The signs of the zodiac

- The archetypal qualities of the 12 signs of the zodiac have long been understood by astrologers. These qualities colour the behaviour of any planet contained within that sign – more strongly if the planet lies towards the centre of the sign.
- The quality of the life similarly changes as the Age Point moves from sign to sign around the chart.

The planets

- The planets, affected by their containing zodiac sign, are seen as operating at three levels of ego, roughly characterised as 'sleeping', 'waking', and 'awake', and at a transformed, spiritual, level. Keywords given below are indicative, not definitive.

- Sun, Moon, Saturn represent the core personality: mind, feelings, body; their glyphs are in red.
- These are also key planets in the Family Model, which reflects the child's (Moon) early experience with mother (Saturn) and father (Sun) figures.
- The inner planets of the solar system represent tools of our personality: Mercury (thinking, communication), Jupiter (perception, expansion), Mars (masculinity, action), Venus (femininity, beauty).
- The outer planets are transpersonal and are of particular spiritual significance: Uranus (research, new systems), Neptune (universal love) and Pluto (transcendence).

The aspects

- Only the 'Ptolemaic' aspects that are multiples of 30° are used, and the degree of tolerance (orb) is Huber-defined.
- Aspects are not drawn to AC, IC, DC, MC.
- The pattern of the aspects is evaluated by the astrological psychologist using both intuitive and analytical methods, harnessing both left- and right-brain.

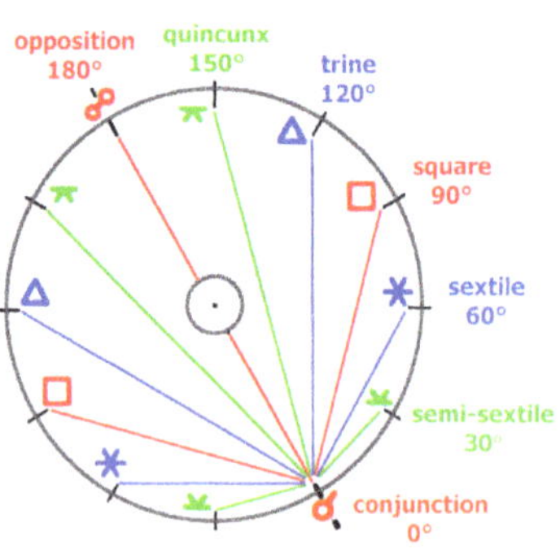

30 degree aspects

Other features

- In this book we show only Natal Charts; the Hubers also use the House Chart, emphasizing environmental demands on the individual, and the Moon Node Chart, depicting karma and the unconscious shadow personality.
- Other special features developed by the Hubers include Stress Planets, Dynamic Calculations, Click Chart, Integration Chart...

Glyphs, Symbols, Colours, Abbreviations

Planetary Glyphs

Sun	☉	♂	Mars
Moon	☽	♃	Jupiter
Saturn	♄	♅	Uranus
Mercury	☿	♆	Neptune
Venus	♀	♇	Pluto

ascending Moon Node ☊

The text also refers to the European symbols for Uranus: ⛢ and Pluto: ♇.

Sign Glyphs

Aries	♈	♎	Libra
Taurus	♉	♏	Scorpio
Gemini	♊	♐	Sagittarius
Cancer	♋	♑	Capricorn
Leo	♌	♒	Aquarius
Virgo	♍	♓	Pisces

Element colours

Sign symbols are coloured by their element.

Fire	= Red	Earth	= Green
Air	= Yellow	Water	= Blue

Abbreviations Used

AC = Ascendant	LP = Low Point
IC = Imum Coeli	BP = Balance Point
DC = Descendant	AP = Age Point
MC = Medium Coeli	

Aspects and Colours

Trine 120°, Sextile 60°	= Blue	△ ✱
Square 90°, Opposition 180°	= Red	□ ☍
Semi-Sextile 30°, Quincunx 150°	= Green	⚺ ⚻
Conjunction 0°	= Orange	☌

The World They Grew Up In

European conflict

From 1914 to 1945 the two world wars and their interregnum saw European conflict on an almost unimaginable scale. Germany was twice defeated by allies, its economy and infrastructure destroyed. Switzerland, on the other hand, had remained studiously neutral, so its citizens fared relatively well, although its economy was badly affected. These were the contrasting environments in which the young Bruno Huber (born 1930 in Switzerland) and Louise Böck[4] (born 1924 in Germany) grew up.

This low-level aerial photograph shows the devastated city centre of Stuttgart in 1945, after 53 major air raids, most of them by Royal Air Force Bomber Command, destroyed nearly 68 percent of its built-up area and killed 4,562 people.[5]

Stuttgart 1945

Louise and her first husband moved there a year later. There was similar destruction to the centre of Bamberg, Louise's town of birth.

Intellectual and spiritual environment

Sue Lewis's extensive research has clarified a number of key intellectual and spiritual influences that were active during the 19/20th centuries[6], and which effectively established the environment within which the Hubers' own development would come to fruition.

4 Louise's maiden name Böck supplied by her granddaughter, Samantha Breno.

5 Photograph of Stuttgart 1945 taken by a member of the allied forces, released by the Imperial War Museum, via Wikimedia Commons.

6 Sue Lewis, *Astrological Psychology, Western Esotericism and the Transpersonal (APWET)*, HopeWell 2015.

Psychology, Spirituality and Astrology

The seeds for a new spirituality were set with the foundation of the Theosophical Society in New York in 1875, and the related writings of its founder Helena Blavatsky. Blavatsky assimilated esoteric streams of West and East, blending them into a universal religion, and elaborating a human constitution including such concepts as karma and reincarnation. Although Blavatsky actually said little about astrology, this laid the foundation for an astrology of self awareness and spiritual growth[7].

Helena Blavatsky
1831-1891

Psychologist William James's *The Varieties of Religious Experience* set the scene for a more spiritual psychology in 1902, and indeed initiated the use of the term 'transpersonal'[8]. Roberto Assagioli later described James's work as 'a model for the impartial scientific investigation' of spiritual consciousness and the superconscious.

William James
1842-1910

Astrologer Alan Leo became a Theosophist, and pioneered the shift from predictive to psychological and spiritual astrology, coining the term 'character is destiny'. He encouraged clients to learn about their own charts, and introduced Western astrologers to many Hindu concepts, including karma and reincarnation. Leo is regarded as the 'father of modern astrology'[9].

Alan Leo
1860-1917

---

7 Nick Campion, *A History of Western Astrology II (AHWA II)*, Continuum UK 2009, page 230.

8 Lewis, Op.Cit. *APWET*, page 31.

9 Lewis, Op.Cit. *APWET*, p. 103; Alan Leo, *The Art of Synthesis*, first pub. 1912.

Esotericist Alice Bailey was first contacted by a Master of Wisdom as a young girl in 1895 and marked out for a spiritual life. She became a member of the Theosophical Society in 1917, but after establishing contact with channelled Master Djwal Khul, broke away and established the Arcane School and Lucis Trust in 1923. The Arcane School is a spiritual school with the keynotes of *service* and *love of humanity*[10]. It has continued ever since. Bailey's many books included *Esoteric Psychology I and II*, and *Esoteric Astrology*[11]. Bailey was largely responsible for popularising the term New Age as a synonym for the Age of Aquarius[12].

Alice Bailey
1880-1949

The early 1900s saw the pioneering of new dimensions of psychology by first Sigmund Freud (1856-1939) in Austria and then Carl Jung (1875-1961) in Switzerland. Key differences leading to Jung's famous split from Freud, that began around 1910, included Jung's recognition of the spiritual nature of humanity and acceptance of astrology[13].

Italian psychologist Roberto Assagioli studied the work of Freud, but soon broke away to follow his own path, around the same time as did Jung. Assagioli conceived his own system of psychosynthesis, which itself became a psychological movement[14]. In 1936 he found common cause with Dane Rudhyar; in their psychotherapy and astrology respectively both sought to help clients achieve synthesis[15]. After the ending of the war, Assagioli established his Psychosynthesis Institute in Florence. Assagioli was also a member of the Arcane School and a friend of Alice Bailey.

Roberto Assagioli
1888-1974

In 1930 Assagioli and Alice Bailey were keynote speakers at a conference in Ascona, precursor to what became regular Eranos

10 Alice Bailey, *The Unfinished Autobiography*, Lucis Trust, 1951

11 Alice Bailey, *Esoteric Psychology I*, 1936, *Esoteric Psychology II*, 1942, *Esoteric Astrology*, 1951, all pub Lucis Trust.

12 Campion, Op.Cit. *AHWA II*, page 241.

13 Campion, Op.Cit. *AHWA II*, page 265.

14 Lewis, Op.Cit. *APWET*, page 29.

15 Lewis, Op.Cit. *APWET*, page 23.

conferences in Switzerland, at which Jung became a leading light. These conferences were oriented towards a spiritual understanding of intellectual ideas, well summarised in the words of Adolph Portmann, quoted by Sue Lewis[16]:

> The Eranos meetings have always aimed to serve the life that exists. Their exploration of archaic traditions of thought has not been for the sake of irrationality per se nor because of any fundamental opposition to... rational attitudes. The reason for cultivating this archaic world view was because it offered a domain where a richer and purer form of harmony exists between rational and irrational experience, and because here the creative powers can bear forceful witness to the vastness of the inner, spiritual realms and to things that have the power to make us whole, things which we are in danger of losing...[17]

Musician Dane Rudhyar first became interested in astrology in 1920 through American theosophists. Subsequently, he studied the astrology of Marc Edmund Jones (1888-1980), became a student of Alice Bailey and immersed himself in Jungian psychology while also writing articles for *American Astrology* in the early 1930s. Bailey's Lucis Press published Rudhyar's seminal work, *The Astrology of Personality* (1936), on what he came to call humanistic astrology, which assimilated character-based astrology and Jungian psychology[18].

Dane Rudhyar
1895-1985

Rudhyar was a progressive thinker who differentiated between the medieval mindset of predictive astrologers and soul-centred modern astrology seeking spiritual development[19].

The ideas of all these key thinkers and more were around in the intellectual ferment of post-war Europe, as the young Bruno and Louise Huber explored the various philosophical, psychological, spiritual and astrological trends, leading to their eventually working with Assagioli and developing the astrological psychology that would become their life's work.

---

16 Lewis, Op.Cit. *APWET*, page 21; Eranos = 'banquet of ideas'.

17. Adolfo Portmann, *Eranos Jahrbuch*, 30 (1961), in Hakl, pp. 11, 295 n. 32 and 33.

18 Dane Rudhyar, *The Astrology of Personality*, 1936; input from Sue Lewis.

19 Campion, Op.Cit. *AHWA II*, page 248.

Early Years

Formation of an esotericist

We have little information on Louise Böck's life growing up in Bamberg, Germany. Louise's mother was Romanian, and Louise had three older sisters and a younger brother. However, the relationship between her parents wasn't good for a long time. When Louise's father divorced her mother she had to live alone until the divorce was finalised. Louise was almost 5 years old when her mother left in the middle of the night to return to Romania. This was really hard for such a young child[20].

Louise's father remarried. Louise's diary suggests that her oldest sister, already aged 18, did not like her stepmother and got all the siblings to make life difficult for the her at first. Louise later said that she grew up in a family of six, so was never alone. In later life she liked having people around: "there were always people living with us[21]".

Louise was growing up during the years of increasing Nazi power. Louise would have been nine when Adolph Hitler became German Chancellor in 1933, and twenty one when her country surrendered to end the war in 1945.

The war took its toll on the family and Louise. Her father died quite early on. Her much loved younger brother went missing in action in Russia at age 18 and was presumed dead. At 20, Louise was deeply in love with a pilot and they planned to marry, but he died in a crash.

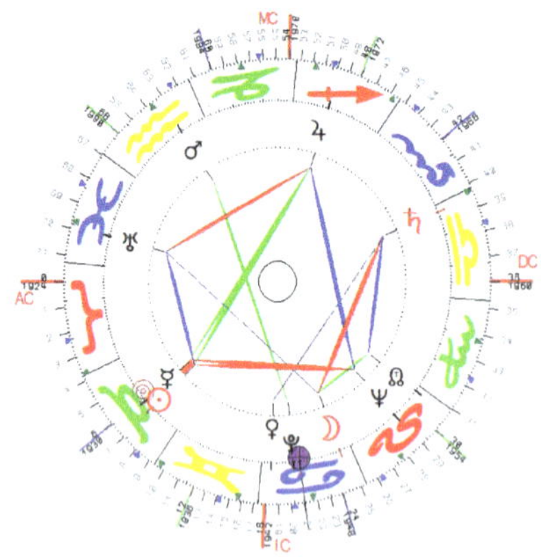

Louise's chart showing AP at 8 May 1945, date of German surrender. AP has just passed over Pluto, planet of transformation.

20 Stories of Louise's early family life supplied by Samantha Breno from family papers. We note that the divorce corresponds with Louise's AP being opposite Saturn, the mother figure in the Family Model.

21 Verena Bachmann, 'Interview with Louise Huber', *Astrologie Heute* 2003, tr. Joan Solé into Spanish then Sue Lewis into English, pub. *Conjunction* 65, May 2016, page 13 on..

Louise later gave some insight into how she perceived her situation, and how she became interested in the esoteric[22]:

> As a result of the Second World War, I suffered four years of war. Initially I wanted to study sports, then everyone was conscripted. First I was in the social service, later serving in the war effort, obliged to work for the Luftwaffe. I was there until the end, when the English made me a prisoner. Then, seeing how the ideology of the Third Reich had failed, I looked deeply into the meaning of life and the essence of being human.
>
> Everything was literally destroyed, and that stimulated my approach to spiritual questions, a thirst for spiritual answers, questions about existence, new ideals. I was then living in Stuttgart, married to my first husband[23], who was interested in spiritual matters and vegetarianism, trying to purify body and soul. In those days, the spiritual elite of Germany lived in Stuttgart, and I was able to attend many conferences. For five years, I attended a conference nearly every day, which was amazing. In this way, I connected with astrology, the Arcane School of Alice Bailey, and other spiritual trends.

Formation of a seeker after truth

Wolfhard König summarises Bruno Huber's early childhood in Switzerland.[24]

> Bruno Huber's early childhood was spent with his parents and sister in Leinbach in the Sihl valley which, at the time, was a largely rural area right outside Zurich. It so happened that young Bruno found himself alone for a fair bit of time, sitting at the window watching the world go by (Moon in Pisces, lst house). This probably set the stage for his pronounced tendency to observe and to reflect.

---

22 ibid.

23 Louise's first husband, Armin, was 16 years older, surname unknown. Information supplied by Samantha Breno.

24 Wolfhard König, 'Bruno Huber, Psychologist and Astrologer', *Conjunction Digest III*, page 57. Written as *Astro Glossarium* entry for Bruno.

Sensitive child

Bruno later explained how he learnt to keep his inner world to himself[25].

> In my childhood I suffered because of my sensitivity. I had a sister, but she was only six years old, and my mother feared something might happen to me if I went out to play in the street with other children. So she moved my bed to the window of my room so that I could look outside but remain under her protection. So I observed the world from the window. This went on for four years.
>
> I wasn't ill, my mother just wanted to protect me, and I learnt to observe. I have clear memories going back to when I was only two years old.
>
> Outside there was a little garden and a street. Of course I couldn't hear what people below were saying but I tried to decipher their conversation, I was fantasizing. When, finally, my mother let me go out to play in the street, evidently, I had no experience of how to relate to the other children and they made fun of me. But whenever a child said something other than s/he really thought, I realized immediately. I don't know why, but I knew for sure it wasn't true. This became ever more obvious… probably it was a preparation for my later work as a psychologist.
>
> From childhood, I learnt to keep my inner world to myself. At that time, things would not otherwise have gone well. As I have always been overly sensitive, I saw and felt things others would not have understood. They'd have said, "he's nuts"! As a result, there was no point in sharing them. For example, once I said to someone with utter frankness that, in reality, he didn't think what he'd just finished

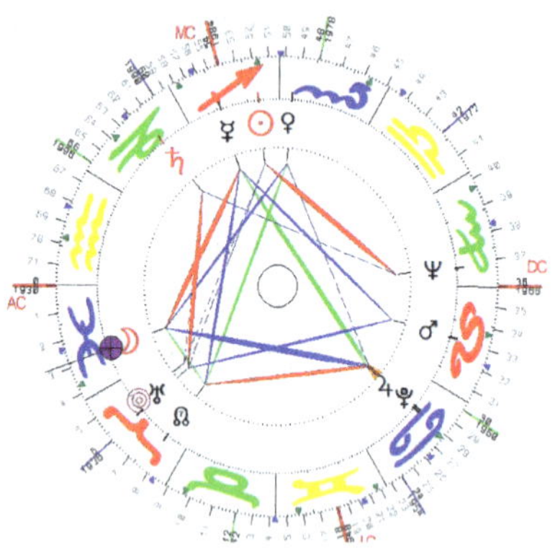

Bruno's chart showing AP conjunct Moon in sensitive Pisces, age 3

25 Verena Bachmann, 'Interview with Bruno Huber', *Astrologie Heute* 82, Dec 1999, tr Joan Solé into Spanish, then Sue Lewis into English.

saying. That guy punched me. So I learnt, from being a boy, to keep my inner world to myself. I have the nature of a hermit. I can spend hours and hours alone without difficulty. I never get bored, nor does the necessity arise for me to be with people.

I was brought up by two women, my sister and my mother. My father appeared from time to time, mostly with his breath smelling of beer. In those times of war and crisis, he had no work and was always seeking employment. For me, he hardly entered into the scene. Only later did I realize that some things in me were inherited from him. He was a good craftsman and sometimes he let me work with him. He taught me how to use tools.

It would seem that Bruno was quite disconnected from his father. We note that, in terms of the Family Model, there is only a very indirect connection in his chart between the Moon and Sun, involving one-way aspects, suggesting just such a tenuous connection with his father.

Teenage years

Wolfhard König continues Bruno's early family story[26]

At 12 the family moved into Zürich, thus beginning a new chapter in his life which gave scope for his extrovert and individualistic side (Sun in Sagittarius, 9th house, and Mercury conjunct MC). He thoroughly enjoyed testing out his leadership qualities and soon became a leader in the boy scout movement, reaching the rank of 'Feldmeister'.

Between ages 14 and 18 Bruno went through a phase of extreme self-searching. He wanted to test his own potential to its limits. He managed to achieve top results in a variety of sports such as cycling, skiing and mountaineering, and a world record in diving. From an astrological point of view this may be explained by Sun and Mars being Low Point planets, which often leads to special efforts, to over-compensate, in order to prove their worth. By the same

Bruno, 1948
photo: family

26 König, Op.Cit. Bruno Huber.

token his revolt against anything to do with school and teachers was equally drastic.

Bruno was an intense `Seeker after Truth' which led him to the study of the sciences at various universities. He developed a special interest in physics and astronomy, and this brought him to astrology and psychology. Sun in the 9th house and Mercury at the MC demonstrate his need to think for himself – also Saturn, Uranus, Mars and Mercury which are all connected to each other by aspect structure.

The square aspect between Uranus and Saturn points to his radical need to challenge the limits imposed by establishments. Bruno rejected all and any exams and career structures lest he find himself trapped within some system or other (for instance he opted out of his Officer training in the Armed Forces). Above all else he valued his chance to be a free thinker and to act according in his own conscience.

Polarities

Late in life, Bruno clarified that he 'discovered the hidden side of human nature extremely early'[27].

> The question of the two sides of human nature, the visible and the invisible, captured my attention exceedingly early. Anyway, I always processed my experiences with considerable inner objectivity. I would ask myself, what is the difference between the impression I have been given and the reality which I know is something else? I always approached these matters scientifically, otherwise I wouldn't have been able to resolve them. When I couldn't explain something, I recorded the question internally and searched for information until I found an answer. I had to learn this skill early on so as not to lose my nerve.
>
> For me it became a most effective working principle: to reflect a few times and seek more information until I found something that really made sense. That was decisive! For me, there was no value in a mental principle that didn't function practically.

27 Bachmann, Op. Cit. Bruno Huber interview.

> In my chart I have five planets on low points and five more close to cusps, hence, introversion and extroversion – two opposite poles are emphasised, which are both important to me.
>
> From childhood, I had a recurrent dream. Above, I saw a bar with elastic bands and hooks hanging from them. And below I saw another bar, also with elastic bands and hooks. In dreams, and also in waking dreams, I always tried to unite the bands above with the bands below. This vision repeated again and again. It was an image that remained with me. I didn't want there to be some hooks hanging and others on the ground that didn't communicate with each other. So when I later developed my conceptual astrological and psychological model, I intended it to be a model of synthesis without lots of disconnected parts. That wasn't easy, above all if it was going to work for the human being.

There is another polarity in Bruno's chart, between fire and water signs. Bruno relates how his mother helped him to handle these contradictory sides of his character:

> My mother passed on to me a principle that is always helpful. When I launch into something too quickly, I'm always reminded: if it gets complicated, sit down and reflect; and when you've finished, reflect again! Thinking stimulates me a lot and for me this is key – not taught thinking, but what I would describe as my own conscious thinking, the kind of thinking I observe myself thinking, just as I observe myself seeing. I try to achieve a high level of rationality in my consciousness and in this way keep the opposites united within.
>
> By means of observation, reflection, and finally application. Checking it works! That also corresponds to the principle of Sagittarius[28], its desire to go beyond.

---

28 Sagittarius is Bruno's Sun Sign.

Atheism and The Jesuits

In young adulthood, after a short period of atheism, Bruno came to be taught by the Jesuits[29].

> I was with the Jesuits and for a time I intended to convert and become a lay Jesuit. I discovered the Jesuits after a phase of atheism during my early years as a student. Their intellectual acumen fascinated me and I was educated by them for two and a half years. That was when I really learnt to think. I also learnt to observe the people I came across so carefully that I could recognize cracks in their thinking, areas where their arguments broke down. We all try to hide these gaps. The Jesuits are specialists at seeing through them.
>
> But ultimately I couldn't accept their authority. To actually become a lay Jesuit, you have to promise absolute obedience. I couldn't do that. We stayed up all night discussing this issue and finally I had to say farewell. For me it closed that chapter for ever. The training of my mental skills during that period was enormously beneficial. But the faith and all that came with it was not for me.
>
> When I left I had to promise them never to say anything against the Catholic Church. The Jesuits watched me for years to make sure I kept that promise. In every class I could recognise one, by their argumentative method.

29 Bachmann, Op. Cit. Bruno Huber interview.

2. Attraction to Astrology

At different times in their lives, both Bruno and Louise Huber set down their own personal reflections on their journey to astrological psychology, and particularly how they came to be fascinated by the subject of astrology. Bruno wrote his account in 1987 when he was just fifty seven; Louise wrote hers in 2004 at the age of eighty. This part of their stories follows.

Louise – Like a Duck to Water

Louise's story comes chronologically first, beginning as it does in the immediate postwar years, when Bruno was still a child[31].

> My interest in astrology was first aroused by a phrase in the book *Horoskopie* by Fankhauser[32], where he talks, among other things, about the "impossibility of salvation for Taurus". I was both fascinated by the expression and angered by its categorical nature. However, it was the reason why I started to study astrology myself, in order to find out whether the statement was true or not. I calmed down later, when I read about Taurus in Alice A. Bailey's book *Esoteric Astrology*. She described the "cosmic bull, who prepares the way for the coming avatar with

Louise as a young woman

31 Louise Huber, article 'The Development of an Astrologer', first published in *Astrolog* 139, 2004, later in English in the APA booklet *The Development of Astrological Psychology (DAP) 2017.*

32 Alfred Fankhauser (1890-1973) was a Swiss writer, poet, journalist and astrologer.

hammer blows", which I much preferred and which inspired me in my later work.

After the War

In 1946, after the end of the war, many things had changed. In Germany, a world had collapsed; the ideals that had driven many young contemporaries to their deaths were cast aside. We had to find a new life with new meaning and new values. When I came to Stuttgart in 1946, I and my first husband lived strictly according to the teachings of Mazdaznan[33]. I escaped completely into the "spiritual life", in order to overcome the difficult experiences of the latter years of the war (1944 in Berlin and subsequent English imprisonment).

At the time, the spiritual elite of defeated Germany had gathered in Stuttgart. I had the freedom and good fortune to be able to attend lectures by experts in their field nearly every day. I made the most of it; for five years I was exposed to the experiences and knowledge of great thinkers. There was Manfred Keyserling, the son of the famous German philosopher, who provided an unbelievably brilliant introduction to the new philosophical ideas. There was Graf Dürckheim, who had a small circle (to which I belonged), where we could have therapeutic discussions with him. There was Dr. Burger-Karis, who specialised in art therapy and therapeutic discussions, Dr Hans Endres who provided introductions to the humanities and there was of course also astrology and the Arcane School, with which I was intensively involved during the five years I spent in Stuttgart.

I learnt astrology from Elisabeth Richter, who gave private lessons to a small group of us in Stuttgart. My first astrology books were by Else Parker from Holland, Karl Brandler-Pracht and Otto Pöllner from Germany, Alfred Fankhauser from Switzerland, who brought the theosophical idea of "the treasures of the spirit" into astrology.

I took to Astrology like a Duck to Water

I was so excited by the possibility of being able to read people's character and destiny from their horoscopes that after just one year's study, I opened my own astrological consultancy in Stuttgart. I wanted to use my knowledge to help as many people as possible and

33 Mazdaznan is a neo-Zoroastrian religion which held that the Earth should be restored to a garden where humanity can cooperate and converse with God.

offered my services with this in mind. I advertised in two so-called occult magazines, in *Die Andere Welt* and in *Die Weisse Fahne*, the official magazine of the Unity-Bewegung. I had many replies. But everything turned out very differently than I had imagined.

There were wives and mothers who wanted to know if their husbands, fathers and sons were still alive, if they were in prison and when they would be coming home. There were calls for help from refugee camps from people wanting to know when they would finally find a home. There were questions from war invalids, who wanted to know if they would still be able to find work without a right arm. I was suddenly confronted with the combined miseries of those sad times. Astrology only seemed to be of interest to those who were suffering or desperate.

Resignation

I kept going for three months. I drew up horoscopes and calculated, reflected, researched and wrote texts for the clients. I looked for passages in books that were relevant to each person's circumstances, but everything was so miserable, inadequate and oracular. I studied and studied to try to find answers, I calculated Moon and axis directions, I went through all the current transits, I tried new Glahn methods, in order to work out the destiny of these poor people. But nothing satisfactory came of it. Sometimes I had sleepless nights because I did not know how I was going to cope. The more I thought about it, the more I needed to know both my own limits and those of traditional astrology. I had to admit that I could not answer such questions with a good conscience, and I closed my office immediately.

Learning Process

During this time I learnt something valuable and very important for my later activities. I discovered that I could help many people much more with just a few comforting and encouraging words, and with compassion and sympathy than with descriptions of star constellations, possible transits or axis directions. And so my interest in psychology and spiritual work began to grow. In 1948 I enrolled in the Arcane School founded by Alice A. Bailey. This is an esoteric correspondence course that I found very challenging on all levels and which kept me busy for the next few years. To begin with, I had trouble following the elevated flights of thought and abstract ideas. However, I had no problem in writing up my monthly lessons and conscientiously doing my daily meditation. Every Arcane School student had an older student as a mentor (secretary). Mine was Frau Anny Huber-Wuhrmann from Zürich, with whom I had a lively correspondence covering many spiritual and philosophical issues.

Bruno – Early Explorations

Bruno tells a story of initial scepticism, fascination, exploration and disillusion[34].

Bruno 1952

I was just under seventeen years old when astrology entered my life. It was my contrariness that made me tackle it in the first place, and it never left me alone after that.

Just think of it, in the very years when we are at odds with ourselves, when ideals and reality don't quite seem to match up in this world of ours, when we are wont to argue with fate, just when we have to decide on the direction of our future career. I had a passionate fascination with the starry sky, and therefore opted for astronomy. But in each lecture one of my professors, with great fervour and getting redder and redder in the face, spent considerable time denouncing astrology in the most adversarial fashion. In my opinion this attitude was in direct contrast to the scientific method. And because I became curious as to just what he found so objectionable in astrology, I went and bought myself a book about it.

34 Bruno Huber, article 'When Someone Makes a Journey', first published in *Astrolog* 41-45, 1987, later in APA booklet *The Development of Astrological Psychology* (DAP), 2017.

How it all started

I remember very vividly how I went into the bookshop, and, feeling guilty, even heretical, asked for astrological textbooks. I was directed to the top shelf in an obscure area of the shop, called "others", and found there the sum-total of all the literature available on astrology in 1947 in the most prestigious bookshop in Zürich. There were some fifteen small blue booklets of Raphael's ephemeris for individual years and a handful of brochures from some distributors in Germany. These were typed on an old machine, on old paper, with old-style print, and written in such convoluted language that at the time I couldn't make head or tail of it. And there was just one well-produced hard-back copy of a book called *Horoskopie* by one Alfred Fankhauser. I must confess the sight of it intrigued me, and it seemed to be written in a straightforward manner. So I decided there and then to buy Fankhauser's book and study it at leisure.

Obviously this was bound to create conflict within me. It was the typical fight between the left and right hemispheres of the brain (I have a Mercury/Moon square in my natal chart.) Who was right: the supposedly rational professor of orthodox astronomy or the anthroposophical journalist Fankhauser with his interest in astrology?

It took my psyche two years of laboured cogitations to come to a decision: I would leave astronomy behind and turn to psychology instead, in the hope that in this way I might gain some fruitful insights into my attempts to get to grips with my fascinating hobby of astrology. For me, from the very beginning those two disciplines ran parallel to each other, and over the years slowly but surely merged into one as a matter of course.

The first few years of my astrological studies were of course quite cumbersome, because during the time of the second world war there was simply no astrological literature to be had anywhere, nor astrological tools. And neither could I find a teacher. Once, after a lecture, I tried to talk to Fankhauser. He said abruptly, "and how long does it take you to calculate and to draw up a chart?" I confessed it took me about two hours, expecting his displeasure. Sure enough, as he was already turning to the next person he just muttered, "wait until you can manage it in twenty minutes, then I'll talk to you." Full stop!

Mercury poisoning

Therefore I had to fathom out most of the techniques painstakingly by myself. Luckily the mathematics side was no problem to me because of my previous studies. Fankhauser only provided Campanus house tables for the latitude of Switzerland, but I managed to calculate the house cusps for the Placidus and Regiomontanus systems for all necessary latitudes. And I was soon rather proud to be able to calculate and to draw all my charts according to these three different house systems.

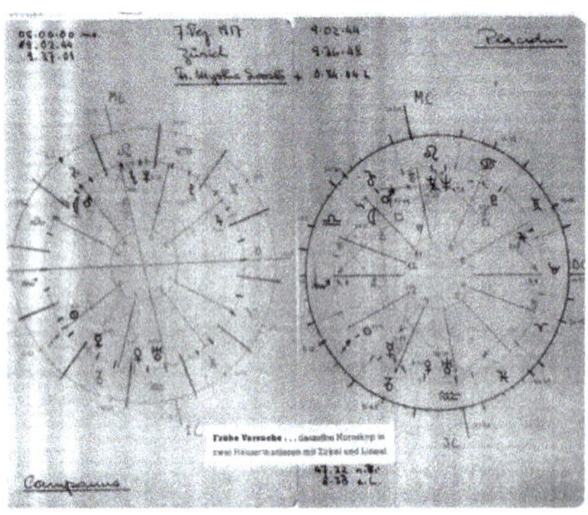

Early charts – Placidus and Campanus

I took to searching around for astrology books in new and secondhand bookshops, and thus managed to acquire a goodly number of useful books, chiefly of the older variety, which I devoured with great gusto. The amount of data that a youthful brain can absorb is quite phenomenal. Within the next three years I managed to take in the views of any number of ancient authors, including Ptolemy, Firmicus, Manilius, Alan Leo, and also the first book by Ebertin. (That's when my Age Point was in opposition to my MC/Mercury[35].) This over-indulgence in technical detail soon brought about a drastic case of mental indigestion. I came to realise that all these different methods only served to

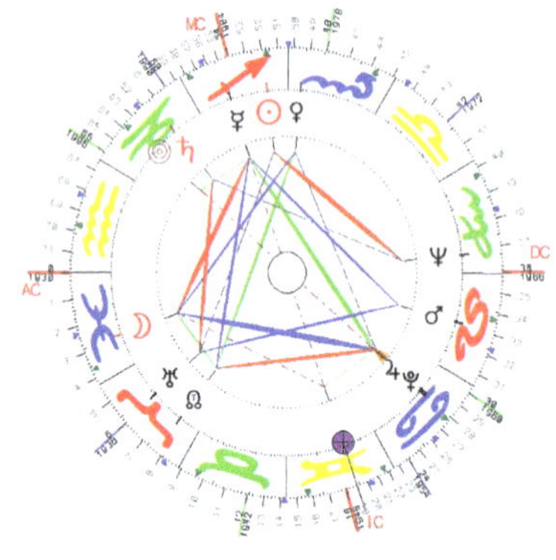

Bruno Huber
showing AP opposite Mercury, 1949

35 Mercury, planet of thinking and the inquiring mind, is activated by the AP opposition at precisely this time of Bruno's life.

confuse me thoroughly, and brought with them a welter of seemingly irreconcilable contradictions. In the end I was overcome by fury and despair about all those crazy astrological constructs. And, in a fit of facing up to the intractability of it all, I determined to put an end to it. I consigned all these tantalising books to the nearest dump, and that was that.

The gestalt within the chart

In any case this was my time to be called up for military service, which is obligatory in Switzerland, and which rather dampened my enthusiasm for everything astrological. For some two years my left hemisphere gave astrology a rest, but the feeling side of my brain couldn't fully let go of it, and I couldn't quite resist the temptation to browse through the several hundred charts that had escaped destruction. These were all charts of people who were known to me personally. Whenever I happened to meet one of them I just couldn't resist the temptation of looking out their chart and having a quick glance at it. Since I was no longer able to look up the meaning of their sign and house positions in one of my cook books, all that was left to me was to brood moodily over those strange configurations. My attention vacillated from their astrological features to their natural facial features, from their astrological patterns to their behavioural patterns...

Nowadays [1987] I realise that something very significant happened within me during that time. I began, at first quite unconsciously, to notice the gestalt within the chart. But I did consciously realise that the visual impact of the charts left much to be desired, as most of them had been dashed down by me in an inordinate intellectual hurry. In those two years I calculated hardly any new horoscopes, but redrew the old ones over and over again, in order to produce a clearer visual impact. And all this brooding over the charts laid the foundations for the newly-to-be-developed method of chart interpretation, one based on reading the aspect figures. This improved technique of pictorial representation highlighted my awareness of the gestalt, but it was to be several more years before the figures yielded their intrinsic meaning.

Near the Low Point

Altogether these two years, between the Balance Point and the Low Point[36] of the fourth house, were the most miserable of my life. My previous bookworm years hadn't just driven me into a blind corner, they had caused me to neglect any personal contact with the outside world, so that I felt intellectually well fed but emotionally starved, old before my years, as I wrote in my diary.

Everything in my life seemed to have come to a full stop. At that time I didn't yet know that the Low Point can feel just like that. But then everything changed.

---

36 Balance Point and Low Point are outlined on page 5. The Low Point often signals a going-inward of energies, presaging change to a new phase of life.

3. Zürich – Partners

1952-56

Meeting and Marriage

Louise's relationship with her Arcane School tutor, Frau Anny Huber-Wuhrmann, was to have significant consequences.

Déjà-vu encounter

Louise tells how Bruno appeared on the doorstep[38].

> In 1952, Bruno came on the scene. He was Frau Anny Huber-Wuhrmann's son, and she sent him on a trip to Germany, hoping that her young son – he was then 22 years old – would be lucky enough to find someone to take him under their wing. So one Sunday morning at 11 o'clock he was standing outside my door in Stuttgart. I opened the door and was naturally very excited to have a visitor from Switzerland. At the time, it was something quite special, and as the son of my spiritual mentor in the Arcane School, we naturally greatly enjoyed each other's company in our two-bedroomed house. For four weeks, we had an intensive exchange of ideas, which went on almost uninterrupted and for nights on end. We established

38 Louise Huber, Op. Cit. *DAP*, page 16.

that astrology, which I had sidelined a little, was a strong link between us, and was both constructive and creative. Bruno's ideas fascinated me, for they were completely different from those that I had hitherto read in books and I already suspected that they contained significant astrological innovations for the New Age.

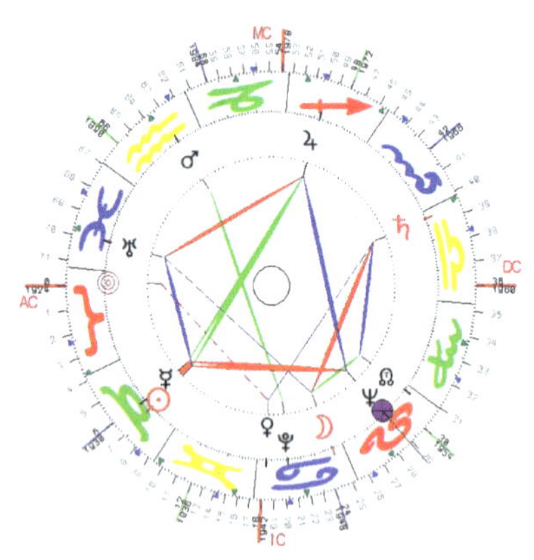

Louise Huber
Showing AP on date of marriage to Bruno. AP is conjunct Neptune.

During the next few years, we were busy with personal matters and had little time for astrology. We were married on 21st March 1953 in Zürich...

Louise is more revealing a later interview[39], their meeting was destiny:

> After all I had heard [in those 5 years in Stuttgart], I had a head full of ideals… I was already married... and then Bruno arrived... He knocked at my door. Meeting with Bruno was the most important turning point of my life.
>
> Bruno stayed at my house for three weeks. We understood each other incredibly well. I shared with him everything I had in my head, transmitted all the knowledge I had accumulated. And he was astoundingly open and receptive. His mother had been a Rosicrucian and student of the Arcane School, and had tried without success to convert him to the spiritual path… which he only came to accept through me.
>
> I didn't know at the time, but up to that point, Bruno had opposed everything esoteric and for a time he had even been an atheist, despite his mother's interest in the esoteric. I didn't know that until some while after. In this opening encounter, Bruno appeared to be for everything esoteric, which was for me an important anchor that united us and convinced me that I should agree to have a relationship with him.

39 Bachmann, Op.Cit. Interview with Louise Huber.

In return, Bruno gave me orientation… his sharp intellect gave him a great capacity for differentiation, and this enabled me to order my burgeoning esoteric knowledge.

Commitment

I am very full-on. When I recognize my task, I give myself to it body and soul. The meeting and spiritual exchange with Bruno signalled joint work. I saw that clearly from the beginning.

Six months before I had a vision in my meditation. I saw myself seated in a class, and two rows ahead was a young man who turned round and looked me in the eyes. When, half a year later, Bruno was standing in the porch of my house, I knew he was the man of my vision. For me, our encounter was an experience of déjà-vu. Incredible! An intense experience.

The fact that half a year before our meeting, when I knew nothing of Bruno's existence, I had received a message through meditation was for me a signal that this was part of the divine plan. And, evidently, I was aligned with my Pluto. In less than three months I separated and remarried. When I want something so clearly signalled, I succeed.

A flash of lightning

Bruno continues his story from the 4th house Low Point[40]. Contrary to Louise, Bruno clearly had a lot of time for astrology during this first Zürich period.

From the Low Point

Everything in my life seemed to have come to a full stop. At that time I didn't yet know that the Low Point can feel just like that. But then everything changed. I did what Sagittarians do best when all seems lost: I collected

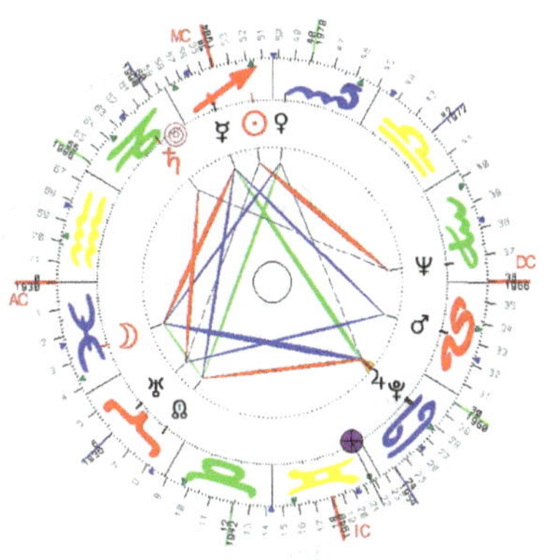

Bruno Huber
AP at 4th house Low Point,
August 1952

40 Bruno Huber, Op. Cit. *DAP*, page 4.

> all my money together, packed my bags, including my tent, and left, direction north. In 1952 hitchhiking was still quite unusual, and I had to rely mainly on my own two feet. After three days I'd got no further than Stuttgart. It turned out that this was in fact the end of this particular journey, but the beginning, as well as the continuation, of quite a different one.
>
> As I was leaving, my mother, who was the secretary of an international esoteric school, had given me a letter to hand to one of her pupils in Stuttgart. It is quite a story to recount just how it came about that I actually hand-delivered this letter to a Mrs. Louise R. Because at the time it seemed to me to be a totally useless activity. In fact it turned out to be the most fruitful one of my whole life. Even as I rang the doorbell I would have preferred to turn tail and go away. But a mere couple of hours later I had no doubt in my mind: this one will be my wife, no one else.
>
> Actually, Louise turned out to be a fanatical vegetarian, and she talked that esoteric gobbledygook which I'd found incomprehensible coming from my mother. But she was an astrologer, and followed with genuine interest all my academic and philosophical musings. And to top it all she was extremely attractive. That was a combination for which I'd looked in women for ages, but up to then had never found it. For me it really was love at first sight. But with Louise, a Taurean, it took a little longer.

Bruno later described this first meeting as[41]:

> Like a flash of lightning in a clear sky. That same afternoon I fell in love. Louise had a most intense presence and glittering armour, probably as a consequence of living through the war. But I could see her golden essence within. Suddenly I knew, this was my wife, the only one. Previously, I had known other women but those relationships had always been like games. They were interesting at the time but later they turned superficial and we began to squabble. In other words, none of them had turned out well. But with Louise it was completely different.

The relationship developed rapidly[42]:

---

41 Bachmann, Op.Cit. Bruno Huber interview.

42 Bruno Huber, Op. Cit. *DAP*, page 4.

The next few days and weeks demonstrated to me how easy it is to learn when we are in love. The more I found out about Louise's esoteric knowledge, the more sensible and convincing it seemed to me, and it explained lots of queries that astrology had raised for me, but which at the time seemed quite inexplicable. Astrology gave us a common language, and the Jupiter/Venus click point[43] in the ninth house of both of our charts worked like mutual mental reinforcement.

The weeks flew by, and we forgot time and space. In endless discussions which never seemed quite long enough we began to formulate the vision of a glorious future together. We envisioned a nobler man in a nobler world, and realised that we both wanted to contribute actively to increasing the quality of human consciousness. And we both understood that to achieve this aim we'd need psychology, philosophy, the sciences, astrology and esoteric knowledge. We even worked out a model for some kind of adult education establishment. Of course we had no idea just how this vision could possibly be turned into reality. We knew that first of all we'd need money and inspiration.

In the spring of 1953, when the Sun was at 0° Aries[44], we stood before the registrar to get married, devoid of any practical ideas on how to make our dreams come true. But we were both filled with the unequivocal desire to dedicate our partnership to the service of mankind.

We now know that these visions of the future already contained within themselves the germs of the idea of the Astrological Psychology Institute as it exists today [i.e. 1987]. But it took years to work this out in practical detail.

1975, 22 years later photo: family

43 Click point: Bruno's Venus is at the same position as Louise's Jupiter in their respective house charts.

44 The spring equinox, at 0° Aries, signals the start of the astrological year.

The Wild Fifties – The Zürich Time

Bruno's story continues with this period of the early fifties in Zürich.

New Astrology

Looking back on the beginnings of my astrological adventure it is fair to say that not only I but the whole of astrology was in limbo at the time of my marriage to Louise. Actually the whole of Europe seemed to be in a Low Point mood after the second world war, and at first made just tentative attempts to resuscitate itself. In the early fifties we saw the hope of economic recovery, and simultaneously a re-awakening of interest in astrology, but astrology with a difference. 1953 saw the publication of new astrology books and the inauguration of new concepts in astrology. Reinhold Ebertin, for instance, with his publishing and multifarious other activities, spearheaded an astrological reawakening.

These new books, plus the many budding lectures and lecturers, stimulated me to give astrology another try. But at the same time there were two other topics that much enhanced my previous interest in astrological studies. They were psychology, which I was studying and which provided me with a new set of tools, and on the other hand philosophy and esoteric studies, with its comprehensive and all-embracing approach.

Actually the so-called New Astrology which now became all the rage made me feel quite uneasy. I devoured all available books and attended all possible lectures, and yet, although there seemed to be many new techniques, the whole attitude was "old hat" to me, based on the medieval assumption that if the stars are in such and such a configuration men react in such and such a way. According to my budding knowledge of astrology this was alright within very narrow limits, it was a description of what might happen, but no explanation. More often than not this was an attitude of fatalism and determinism, "It's all due to the stars, accept your fate, and that's all there is to it."

Needless to say, I used this time to embark on my first series of detailed investigations, questioning rules as propounded in cook books and comparing them with actual facts, devising a series of tests for this purpose. The results of these tests almost invariably proved

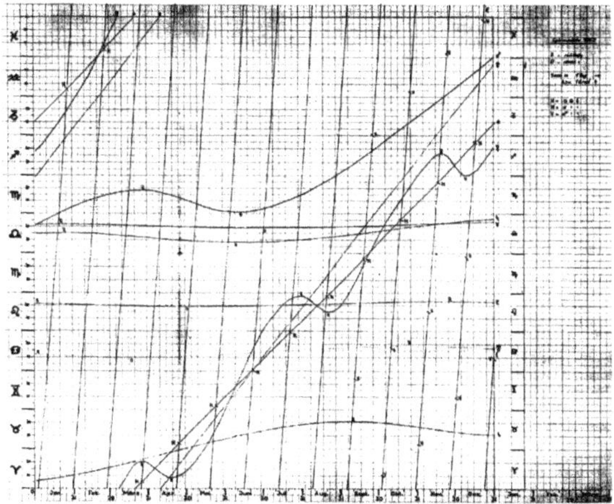

Graph of planetary positions for 1952, drawn by Bruno, giving a quick overview for work with transits.

to be either meaningless or downright disastrous. Until I finally realised that the languages of astrology and psychology really didn't have much in common, as they had different historical backgrounds. They based themselves on different assumptions, grew out of different paradigms, which gave their words different meanings and a different flavour.

The Esoteric

In the end it was the ancient wisdom which provided me with the most fruitful approach to research into astrology. Esotericists explore the underlying structure and the intent which underpin the outward phenomenal appearance of life. That's how they hope to gain a glimpse of the pattern and purpose of nature's ways. This means that from a practical and existential point of view a person's mere behaviour can be quite insignificant, as it can be conditioned by external influences of the society in which they live. Similar behaviour as seen in a number of different people can in fact be the result of very dissimilar motivation. And as long as we don't differentiate between an outward action and the underlying motivation we can't really help people to tackle these underlying issues, only describe them. The best we can hope to do is to reprogramme their behaviour patterns.

In the fifties both Louise and I engaged in an extensive study of the ancient wisdom (Theosophy and Alice Bailey's Arcane School.) This helped us to gain the ever clearer insight that astrology is in fact based on the esoteric mode of thinking, the esoteric paradigm. The way the chart is constructed already tells that it has a holistic approach to human nature. And the ever new combination and recombination of the symbols involved is nothing if not the building of new models of organisation, systems, which are so varied and variable that they can evoke a veritable multiplicity of character traits and modes of behaviour.

The Zürich Time

The years from 1953-56, which we now call the Zürich Time, the first years we were able to spend together, turned into an adventurous exploration of the mental and spiritual thinking of the time, a tentative attempt to gain an overview of the various disciplines, and an endeavour to sample as many as possible of the various humanistic and transpersonal modes of thinking. Our active participation in lectures and our co-operation with various groups enabled us to forge a lot of personal contacts which proved very fruitful. For instance, we regularly attended the meditation sessions of the Arcane School in Zürich, soon became responsible for technical arrangements and the library, gave lectures of our own, and in this way met all the leading lights of the School.

In fact we soon formed deep and lasting friendships with them. And the regular group meetings, which met more and more frequently at our place, more often than not turned into night-long discussions about God and the Universe. We dealt with just about everything that came our way. From graphology to phrenology to astrology, from Chinese horoscopes to acupressure to Zen Buddhism, from a study of Trappist thought to Giordano Bruno's *Eroici Furori*, to Dante's *Inferno* to the Greek concept of catharsis, from Szondi's tests of character and fate, to Spinoza's philosophy, to devout contemplation of *The Verses of Dzyan* of the secret wisdom teachings. We discussed psychological methodologies and spiritual exercises, subjected each other to many tests, both sensible and futile ones, and engaged in an early form of group therapy.

With all this discussing and probing, our mere material existence received short shrift, so of course we were frequently extremely hard up. Every now and then we'd hastily get any sort of job just to keep the wolf from the door, but always for as short a time as possible, so as to be free to concentrate on those aspects of life we deemed important. This of course went very much against the grain of the existing bourgeois ethos.

It was this Zürich Time which enabled me to cut myself totally free from the old classical concept of astrology. Instead, since 1955, I did a lot of research into the basic assumptions of astrology, based on the stimulating ideas mentioned above and with the help of carefully chosen psychological tests, I managed to formulate unambiguous meanings of signs, houses, planets and the seven most important aspects. Thus evidently I achieved something which so far had never actually been attempted in astrology. This painstaking research allowed me to postulate a sound basis which in turn made it easier to correlate astrological findings with psychology. And it formed the springboard for the later-to-be-developed methodologies which now are known as "Huber". They still constitute the groundwork and basic assumptions of our teaching. And most probably they are the main reasons for the success of our School.

The year 1955 was creative not just on the mental and spiritual levels, it also saw the birth of our son Michael-Alexander. My Age Point at the time had reached the opposition to Saturn in the 11th house, with a square to Uranus in the second[45]!

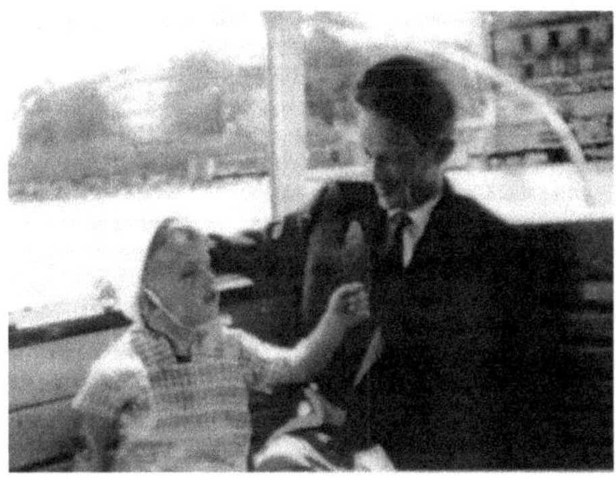

Bruno with son Michael

45 Bruno's AP in the nurturing sign of Cancer in the creative 5th house aptly expressed Bruno's new role as a father bringing with it responsibilities (Saturn in opposition) and highlighting the difficulties of erratic earning with Uranus in the 2nd house.

The following table is an example of the way in which I painstakingly worked out the intrinsic meaning of astrological concepts.

The Aspects		
Impulse, encounter bondings	☌	0°
Friction hardening, crystallisation	□	90°
Resistance, tension, negative engagement	☍	180°
Harmonious growth	⚹	60°
Perfection, completion	△	120°
Embryonic hesitant beginnings	⚺	30°
Duality, split motives decision crisis	⚻	150°

General		
Red	duality	tense, hard, definitive, apparently unalterable
Blue	unity	relaxed, calm,gentle, mobile, adaptable
Green	plurality	hesitant, seeking, undecided

Working Hypothesis for the Aspects, 1955

4. Geneva – the Esoteric

1956-1958

The link with the Arcane School through their involvement in the local Zürich group proved decisive in determining the next stage of the Bruno & Louise's lives. They were asked to spend three years helping to establish a new centre for the Arcane School in Geneva, complementing the centres already established in London and New York. At the same time they were caring for their young baby.

Difficult times

Louise explains that was not easy to make the move to Geneva[47,48]:

> In 1956, when Michael was 8 months old, we were called to Geneva to help build the third main centre of the Arcane School. We were only initially guaranteed a salary of 360 Swiss francs per month for three months. We had to burn our boats in Zürich, and our friends said we were mad to leave everything for three months of work.
>
> The decision to go to Geneva was very difficult, above all for me because I am a Taurean. It meant leaving everything that was secure and leaping into the void.
>
> These were very difficult times for us, as this type of organisation lacked funds. We lived on donations; from hand to mouth, so to speak. There was no security. However, I was very enthusiastic about my work at the Arcane School; I was able to handle all the correspondence, and again there were descriptive and influential letters on spiritual development, which gave me a lot of feedback and which helped to enhance my reputation.
>
> After those three months new possibilities came up and, finally, we stayed there for three years.

---

47 Bachmann, Op.Cit. Interview with Louise Huber.

48 Louise Huber, Op.Cit. *DAP*, page 16.

Work for spiritual ideals

Bruno gives his perspective on the time in Geneva and his explorations into esoteric astrology[49].

> In the summer of 1956 we moved to Geneva, called there by the Arcane School to help with establishing a third headquarters, the European Centre. Our life in Zürich seems to have persuaded them that we were capable of this job. The wages weren't very good, and couldn't be guaranteed for any length of time. But for us it was more important that we had been offered our dream job, to work for spiritual ideals. After all, we were quite used to rough it a bit for the sake of our ideals. It turned out to be a very important time for us.
>
> ### Astrology
>
> Astrology had to take a back seat during this time, especially with regard to research. Instead, the formation of an international spiritual school offered a wealth of new and highly interesting contacts. The pupils came from eight different language areas. We made contact with people who worked for one or other branch of UNO, and came from any number of different countries. It made us mentally very adaptive to have access to such an international population, and we became used to conversing in several foreign languages. Added to this was our ever deeper immersion in esoteric philosophy and a variety of meditation techniques. And I only realised later on that, as an apparent side effect, my astrology gained a lot of valid experience, as I was able to draw up the charts of many of these interesting people, and was then able to compare them with their living reality.
>
> There was also another aspect of astrology that caught my imagination and made a considerable impact on me. It was provoked by one of Alice Bailey's twenty books, *Esoteric Astrology*[50]. I seldom study a book from beginning to end, but I did it here, with dubious results. It fascinated me so much because it was totally different from any other book I had read so far. Everything I read I translated into drawings and diagrams. That's how I always worked when I found concepts difficult to grasp. But in this case it didn't really give me a lot that I could incorporate into my own studies. Finally I came to the conclusion that I must be lacking in the required thinking

49 Bruno Huber, Op. Cit. *DAP*, page 7.

50 Alice Bailey, *Esoteric Astrology*, Lucis Press 1951.

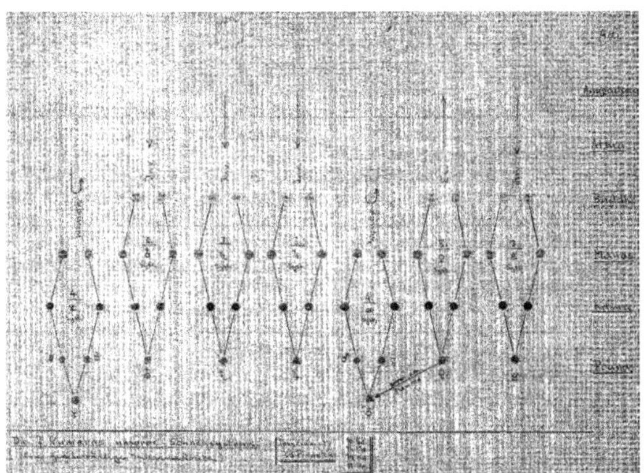

All 49 planets of the solar system, as stipulated by Alice Bailey, on various levels. My own diagram.

apparatus, and put it all to one side, although my self-esteem suffered a bit of a knock through it.

The three charts

Only some twenty years later I suddenly came across a reference from *A Treatise on White Magic*[51], which I actually remembered and understood only then. A.A.B. stated that the astrology of the future would deal with three charts of the same person, which give great depth to the process of interpretation. One chart would be built around the Moon, one around the Sun, and one around the ascendant. In my time in Geneva this meant nothing to me. But at some time in the seventies it suddenly struck me that the Moon Node Chart, and the House Chart, together with the Natal Chart, the method which I had evolved, fulfilled these conditions precisely, not only in the technical definition but also with A.A.B's interpretation that one would represent the past, one the present, and the third the future.

This is the sort of thing that can happen to any explorer and researcher. And it teaches us to be a bit more respectful with that much-prized intellect of ours. Similar occurrences have happened to me frequently over the years in astrology.

51 Bruno originally refers to Alice Bailey's *Esoteric Astrology*, but I think this reference is to *A Treatise on White Magic*, Lucis Press 1934, page 439.

Top-heavy

After about two years of these strenuous, highly spiritual activities in Geneva the psychologist within me began to show withdrawal symptoms. The contact with the pupils seemed to get more and more abstract, distant, and sterile. Occasionally it happened that individual pupils concentrated too much on their meditation exercises and started to show psychic problems; when this happened their tutors invariably advised them to become more detached in their attitude. Obviously this was the official policy of the School. Whenever I tried to increase these pupils' psychological awareness and encourage them to face up to their displacement manoeuvres the top administrators invariably tried to block me.

Significance of this period in Geneva

The importance of this period in Geneva and its focus on the esoteric is suggested by Bruno's thoughts about astrology many years later[52]:

> Astrology is an expression, and I would say the foremost expression, of esoteric thinking. There is no other discipline that comes near to that complete usage of esoteric thinking that astrology does. And I know a lot of disciplines, having gone through most of them in my younger years. None of them is in a similar way absolutely pervaded with spiritual principles.

For Louise, this period had a lifetime's practical impact[53]:

> In the Arcane School, students are encouraged to meditate for 20 minutes every morning to establish contact with the divine plan. I had a lot of practice. and still meditate every day. If I didn't I could hardly live. Here I am once again showing the tenacious side of my Taurus Sun. Once I have recognized something is important, I do it every day. I sit outside on my balcony so as to feel united with nature, which is of great importance to me. The forces of nature flow towards me and, in this way, I replenish my resources. I have been doing this every day for 60 years. Continuity keeps the channel pure and full of vitality… Before meditating, I always say, "I must refresh my channel once again to keep it open."

---

52 Bruno & Louise Huber, *Astrology and the Seven Rays*, HopeWell 2006, page 17.
53 Bachmann, Op.Cit. Interview with Louise Huber.

5. Florence – Psychosynthesis

1959-1962

An Invitation to Florence

Bruno's time in Geneva came to an end after two years, brought to a head by his disagreement with the School on the way to psychologically help people. The opportunity came up for him to visit and help Roberto Assagioli at his Psychosynthesis Institute in Florence. Assagioli was involved with the Arcane School in Zürich, so would have been aware of the young couple and their situation.

A cycling adventure

Bruno tells the story of his first visit to Florence[55].

> In the early spring of 1958, by way of a release, I was hit by a psychological whirlwind from Florence. Professor Roberto Assagioli, whom we had met in Zürich, invited us to take part in a seminar in August on Psychosynthesis. And of course I wanted to go. I had once again developed itchy feet. But we simply didn't have the money for such a long journey, which made me want to go even more. And thus it came about that once again, complete with rucksack and tent, I got on my trusted bicycle, and, with my own muscle power, covered the 700 kilometres to Arezzo, across the Alps over a 2500 metre high pass, and across the plain of the river Po with its searing heat. I was still oblivious of the fact that I had yet again reached a Low Point in my chart, on 15th August 1958 (5th house), and yet again starting a totally new phase of my life[56]. The seminar was supposed to keep me

55 Bruno Huber, Op. Cit. *DAP*, page 7.

56 Bruno does not mention this here, but his Age Point is just passing over the conjunction of Jupiter and Pluto at this point, which is indicative of personal transformation and growth.

in Italy for a mere three weeks. But it opened the door to the most dramatic experiences of my life, and to its most decisive phase of learning and growth.

Spirituality and Reality

After those two years of concentrated highly spiritual work at the Arcane School Centre in Geneva, the contrast of the physical workout on the bike did me the power of good. True, it was a long ride from Geneva to Florence, relying totally on muscle power. And it was my first visit to Italy, and my first experience of its climate in August. In my ignorance, I suffered extensive sunburn all over my body, which had been protected from the outside world for so long. This brought me back to reality with a jolt, a salutary experience which I still remember vividly.

My destination was Capolona, a small village in the Casentino region, near Arezzo, about 100 kilometres south of Florence. Here was Professor Assagioli's summer residence. The camp for psychosynthesis was scheduled to take place in these extensive grounds. I have to confess that I don't retain a clear memory of the seminar which had been the purpose of my trip. The lectures and seminars and the experts from all over the globe have shrunk to mere shadows, like faded holiday snaps. What evoked a really strong psychic and mental reaction in me was the personality of Roberto Assagioli, his library in which I spent many a happy hour looking for spiritual treasure, the countryside surrounding the manse, and the surrounding area which I explored with my bicycle.

Bruno's photograph of Casentino

Low Point Experience

This special blend of an exceptional personality, a wealth of new ideas and compelling natural scenery evoked in me an almost total breakdown of my then existing world view. I vacillated between emotional troughs in which I questioned the meaning of my very existence, followed by mental and spiritual highs. Visions of the future alternated with déja-vu experiences, and even with flash-backs to previous lives. After a week of this I felt totally confused (after all, I had arrived exactly at the Low Point of the 5th house[57].) There was just one thing I knew for certain: my life in Geneva had lost its meaning for me, but what would I do instead?

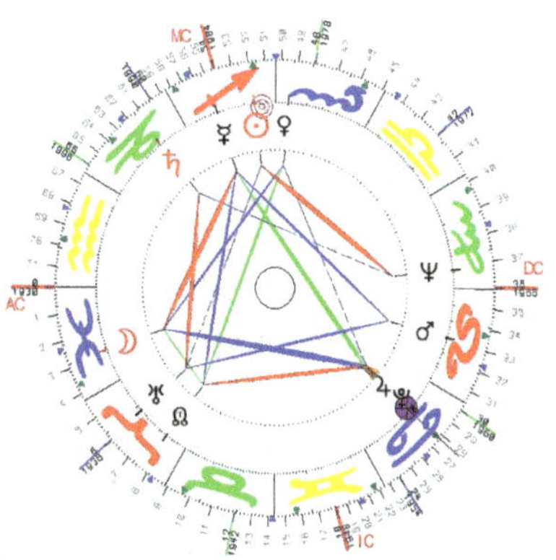

Bruno Huber
AP at 5th house Low Point,
August 1958

The disappearance

During this time, Bruno had a profound spiritual experience which for many years was kept to a close circle of friends, to avoid discrediting him as a psychologist and astrologer, much as Assagioli had years before avoided using the loaded word ‘spiritual’, using the term ‘transpersonal’ instead, to avoid giving the wrong impressions to the ‘scientific’ psychological community. Here Bruno relates the story[58]:

> When I was alone, I had visions that affected me profoundly and turned my life around, so I moved away from an academic way of thinking that had clearly predominated for me until then. I disappeared for two days. I was sitting in the park, I had been meditating… and suddenly I disappeared! They searched for me but didn't find me until two days had passed. Two days later I reappeared in the same place. It was an intense meeting with the unearthly.

57 The Low Point experience is usually particularly deep in the fixed houses 2,5,8,11. This was a life-changing experience for Bruno.

58 Bachmann, Op. Cit. Bruno Huber interview.

Bruno told this story several times, and said verbally that his visions were beyond words, but that he saw all the past and future of humanity laid out before him...

Assagioli's papers

Bruno's narrative continues[59].

> Now the function of the Low Point in a fixed house became apparent, we have to accept the fact that we are stuck and can't see a fruitful way forwards. We meet with gentle pointers provided by the reality of the world around us. In this case I had put it in motion myself, quite unconsciously. My searching in the library had in fact uncovered a considerable number of jottings in Assagioli's own handwriting. They were casually placed in various books and then forgotten. Roberto Assagioli had no idea what wealth of wisdom he had hidden in his books. Occasionally he had tried to retrieve one or other of these notes, but had seldom been successful. And therefore he was very pleased that I had actually found them. He asked whether I might be willing and able to tidy up his books, and to collect his various writings. He'd gladly pay for my train ticket home to save me some travelling time.
>
> I was very intrigued by the prospect of investigating his writings, and not any too keen to pedal along the highways, and catch more sunburn. So I stayed an extra two weeks. The result of my bookworm activities so impressed Roberto that he suggested I should stay on and help him to write a book for which the Psychosynthesis Research Foundation in America had been asking for some time. The result of these negotiations with the Foundation resulted in both of us, Louise and myself, being offered stable positions as Assistant/ Secretary.

59 Bruno Huber, Op.Cit. *DAP*.

The Psychosynthesis Institute

Thus Bruno & Louise moved to Florence to help Roberto Assagioli at his Psychosynthesis Institute. We can again read their own stories.

With Roberto Assagioli

Louise's summarises their time with the wise inventor of psychosynthesis[60].

> Bruno then came into contact with Roberto Assagioli, who invited us to Florence in 1958 after a short dissociation crisis from the Arcane School. We were to help him to write his book *Psychosynthesis Techniques*. In Florence and Capolona we had enough time to make contacts with interesting people. There were artists from Italy, psychologists from America, people from all over the world who had made pilgrimages to obtain help from Roberto Assagioli. Our task was to take care of these people. A group of intelligent young researchers was formed, with which we then also practiced astrology.
>
> **Astrological-Psychological Research**
>
> Roberto Assagioli had a very benevolent attitude toward this venture. We kept him informed about the newest discoveries and findings of our all-night group meetings, and he was very impressed, particularly by the aspect pattern drawings that Bruno was developing at that time. This is how he came to commission Bruno to undertake some fundamental new astrological research, so that this ancient science could finally find a credible place in psychological practice. We not only drew up horoscopes for all participants, but Assagioli made his extensive case file available to us. That was naturally a rich source of information and a productive area for research. He gave Bruno sufficient time for research while I carried on typing up the book on psychosynthesis. Bruno threw himself wholeheartedly into his research work. Bruno had the intelligent group members on his side, as well as Roberto's support. He discovered new things every day and kept the group on their toes with his findings. He motivated them constantly to test out his new discoveries at first hand. We also did the same, and there were critical discussions, doubts, tests, and finally Assagioli was always there, to give us the benefit of his worldly wisdom.

---

60 Louise Huber, *DAP*, page 17.

In a later interview Louise gave a little more information[61]:

> In Florence we found a tremendously stimulating spiritual environment. Every morning at 10:00 we had a group meditation with Assagioli, we participated in group therapy sessions, Bruno discovered colour dialogue and marvellous images emerged. Through working on the book, researching the houses using Assagioli's archive of client cases, and contact with patients, we both made great progress.

Astrology and Psychology

Bruno describes their time at the Psychosynthesis Institute[62].

> So in February of 1959 we moved with child and chattel, with the help of railway containers. Here were the headquarters of the *Istituto di Psicosintesi* and also the winter quarters of the Assagiolis. In summer, because of the sweltering heat in Florence, they escaped to Capolona.

The Park in Capolona. Meeting point of the whole world. Here there are four nationalities, Swiss, German, South African and Californian (U.S.A.)

> Here we began to lead a totally different life. So much happened within the next three years that it is difficult to recount it all in a semblance of order. The intensive involvement with Roberto's patients; personal friendships with people from all over the globe; learning and practising the people-friendly (and very successful)

61 Bachmann, Op.Cit. Interview with Louise Huber.

62 Bruno Huber, Op.Cit. *DAP*, page 7.

therapy called psychosynthesis. Working under the wings of a truly wise person, whose jovial charisma withstood the drag of daily routine and of living and working together. The quite unforeseen possibilities of research into the basic tenets of astrology, which resulted from Roberto's encouragement and support; being immersed in the world of art; the new and the old town of Florence, steeped in culture. And experiencing a Tuscan way of life in an area (Capolona in Casentino) which, for the past 4000 years, has been cultivated with olive trees and vines and where had lived such significant people as for instance Guido di Arezzo, 9th century, who invented the writing of music, Francis of Assisi, who became St. Francis in La Verna, Francesco Petrarca, poet and philosopher, and Piero della Francesca, painter and art critic, pupil of Masaccio, and, and, and...

Work at the Institute

In the Institute we had two main tasks.

We were busy with compiling the textbook of psychosynthesis. For this we had to collect the various papers and essays Assagioli had written over the years on a number of psychosynthesis themes and methods. We had to collect them, put them in order, edit and modify them, at times translate them from Italian and German into English, at times augment them from taped interviews or transcripts. That was a lot of work, and Louise, I have to admit it and record it here with due thanks, did the lion's share of it.

On the other hand a task arose from Roberto's clinical work. It evolved quite naturally, without our having been told to do so. At the time we called it aftercare, follow-on therapy. Assagioli's clients came from all five continents, for therapy sessions lasting from 3 to 5 weeks. He gave them a daily consultation of about 50 minutes. The rest of the day they spent in our vicinity. They didn't rightly know what to do with their time, and were brim full of problems. So we turned into parent-confessors and occupational therapists. Quite often

Bruno assisting at Assagioli seminar

Louise had to cook for them, and occasionally they even slept at our house, especially in Capolona. Sometimes the house was so full that of necessity we had to develop a form of group therapy – something which at the time was quite unknown in therapeutic circles. All this was for us a process of concentrated schooling in psychotherapy. We learned a tremendous lot, and discovered new ways of conducting therapy, which we were then able to discuss and share with Roberto. This in turn enriched his budding book.

Astrological-Psychological Research

Bruno and Assagioli

Bruno recounts the story of some of his research and conclusions during this fertile period[63].

Thus our days were well filled with these activities. And in the evenings I was more and more occupied with basic research into astrology. It was Roberto Assagioli who encouraged me in this, in fact he almost ordered me to do it. Because his own attempts to make sense of astrology had come a cropper, because he found that most astrological literature was full of contradictions and psychologically superficial, and, as he was wont to say, catastrophically inappropriate and helplessly antiquated.

I had told Roberto about my research during the Zürich Time and about my basic definitions. He thought they were a lot more useful than anything else he'd come across in the astrological literature. And he could give me sensible tips for further work. From a psychological point of view he felt that all people had the same basic abilities, based on their common humanity. But each individual was given a slightly different combination of these possibilities, and in different proportions, which explained our individuality. He saw our basic potential in the planets, and thought that here the relevant definitions could be very useful. But what was lacking in his opinion were reliable and unambiguous rules for interpretation, so that we could select the individually appropriate statements for a chart. Which means that for each planet we should be able to determine its effective strength

63 Bruno Huber, Op.Cit. *DAP*, page 7.

within a chart. But both Assagioli's and my own attempts to work this out with the existing rules came to nothing, as the classical rules for the strengths and weaknesses of a planet simply did not coincide with the actual case histories of the individuals concerned.

Research – the houses

These discussions formed in me the concept for my as yet most comprehensive examination – of the house systems. Here and there in astrological literature I'd found attempts to tackle this problem which I had found to be quite hopeful. These were statements suggesting that planets near the cusp of a house were stronger in their effect than in other positions. But how near was near? Different authors quoted different orbs. Some said the effect was only noticeable when planets were placed after the cusp, others stated that planets before the cusp were just as strong. I deduced from this that the house cusp definitely was the strongest possible position. And consequently I began to look for the weakest area in each house.

At that time I hadn't yet made up my mind which house system was the best available, and I always worked with the three different methods, Campanus, Placidus and Koch, and had to conduct all the work three times over. Roberto granted me access to the archives of the institute where I found a great number of case histories which were liberally annotated. I selected those people whose exact time of birth I was able to obtain and whom I could interview personally to check on the results. The project took me all of two years, but yielded three-fold results, much beyond my expectations.

First of all I developed the principle of the House Chart in an attempt to measure precisely the position of the planets at the cusps. I didn't realise its therapeutic meaning until some fifteen years later, with the help of my son Michael.

Then I found the Dynamic Energy Curve which demonstrates the extent of strength available to a planet within the houses. It looks like a sine curve which is asymmetrical and revolves around the Low Point, positioned at the place of the golden mean.

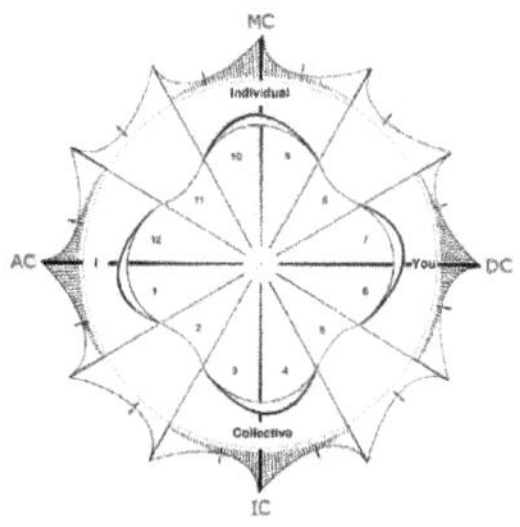

Dynamic Energy Curve

And thirdly I found the only house system suitable for depth psychology and psychosynthesis work, because only the Koch House system corresponded correctly with my measurements and resulted in the above-mentioned unambiguous curve.

Coincidence – the Age Point

The above insights were the result of systematic, long-winded and laborious research, but the next insight resulted by chance, from the apparently coincidental clumping of a special condition. When I worked on the concept of the Age Point I really formed the impression that Fate wanted to demonstrate a specific point to me. For suddenly, in the summer of 1961, our therapy work presented us with fifteen similar cases within the space of a few weeks.

Job related nervous crises, stomach ulcers, giving up the job altogether (the word drop-out wasn't yet known at that time) or very simply a deep dissatisfaction with the job, or failing at work and being helpless, etc. All troubles related to work. Where would astrologers look in the chart? Obviously in the first instance to the sixth house, or perhaps the tenth[64]. Some had planets in those positions, but with most of them there was nothing much to see. And then I suddenly realised a strange factor common to almost all of them. Most of them were at the beginning of their mid thirties, and most of them had a cusp of a sign in their sixth house. At 30 we reckon to be in the middle of our life span. Did the facts point to an involvement with Time? I began to count, with figures between 60 and 100, to find out a hypothetical average life span.

Finally I found out that, if I divided the space between house cusp 6 and house cusp 7 into 72 years, then the end of the sign in the various charts invariably fell in the year which corresponded to the actual age of the native. Eureka, there was a clock ticking away in the sixth house. Then I tried other cases, and other houses corresponding to other themes – and found out that each house had a similar life clock. That was the birth of the small age point. And then came a compelling conclusion: As above, so below, as in part, so in the

---

64 The 6th house is the house of everyday work and service, so this would be the natural place to look for job-related crises. The 10th house relates to power, influence and position in society, so would be another possibility, as Bruno indicates.

whole. I applied the 72 years idea to the whole of the chart. And then it just demanded a bit more hard work to ascertain that the big Age Point actually worked.

It is times like this in the life of an astrologer which almost take your breath away...

Colour, Art and the Spiritual

Colour and painting

Assagioli's Institute attracted a talented collection of international visitors, which opened up a whole new dimension of colour and painting to Bruno[65]:

> By chance I discovered the importance of colour, together with a client, a portrait painter who experienced a crisis of creativity. Whenever, in individual or group therapy, the theme of "father" came to the fore, he just blocked and clammed up. So, in sheer desperation, one evening I suggested to him that we should communicate in colours and not in words. (I myself had just started painting at that time.) We worked together for many an enjoyable hour, and days later it became apparent that his blockage had vanished, once and for all. Today [1987] he is a well-known abstract painter.

Two artists in the convent "La Verna".
On the right is my friend Jim, to whom I owe the discovery of speaking with colours.

---

65 Bruno Huber, Op.Cit. *DAP*, page 7.

Venus poisoning

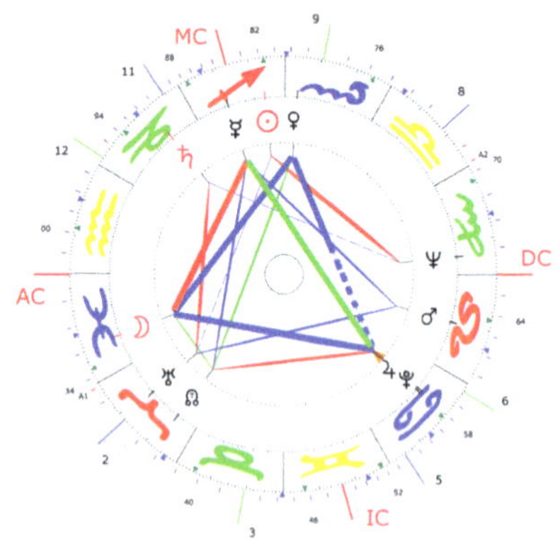

Bruno's chart with Learning Triangle and Large Talent triangle highlighted

Whilst in Florence I developed a passionate love affair which was impossible to dislodge, and which had strange side effects on my career in astrology. I knew that I contained contradictory traits of the scientist and the artist. No doubt this can be traced back to a double figure in my chart. I have two large triangles built on the base of the trine between the first house Pisces Moon and the Jupiter/Pluto conjunction at the Low Point of the 5th house (the very constellation which brought me to Florence – see above.) Mercury at the MC forms a Dominant Learning triangle whilst Venus at the cusp of the 9th house forms a somewhat weaker Large Talent triangle on the same base .

Therefore I work mainly via the intellect (Mercury) but can't avoid the occasional artistic bout (Venus) whenever outward stimuli become sufficiently potent. Here in Florence, the capital of the Renaissance movement, it was bound to happen. During the time in Zürich I had tried becoming a photographer. But this time a group of American painters (Fulbright scholars) who called on us quite regularly released in me an urge to paint which I just couldn't resist. And so, after the first few tentative steps, and with all my other manifold activities, I began to paint abstracts, like a man possessed.

Only a few years later did my Mercury, the researcher, make me realise that I produced a painting at each full moon and each new moon, precisely, and at no other time. And what's more, the pictures invariably dealt with the quality of the sign concerned. This caused a lot of pride for my artistic self, and in due course I agreed that an esoteric friend of mine organise an exhibition of my work in London. And people pounced upon the pictures and wanted to buy them. But I simply couldn't bring myself to part with them, so I increased the price tenfold – and that was that.

> By now I have only a small number left of this first-year series, because I just gave the pictures away with a glad heart to a friend or even a patient, if they particularly liked them. What a pity, says my Mercury, because the complete series would be of considerable interest from an astrological and even a scientific point of view.

Wolfhard König, a close collaborator of Bruno's adds[66]:

> Contact with the American painters made Bruno realise the importance of colour, with its special therapeutic qualities and possibilities for self understanding, and which nowadays is used in art therapy and Gestalt work.

These experiences provided the basis for the workshops on 'colour dialogue' that later became a regular feature of API summer schools, usually involving Wolfhard as well as Bruno.

1993, Achberg, Bruno & Louise dancing
Students' work with colour dialogue is on the walls

photo: family

The Spiritual in Art

Sue Lewis has researched the artistic side of Bruno & Louise's time in Florence and describes elegantly their experience and its effect on the visual image of Bruno's subsequent design of the birth chart[67]:

> Bruno and Louise were bowled over by Florence, especially Bruno, who discovered the language of colour from the American Fulbright art scholars he met there. So he read Goethe's *Theory of Colours* (1810)

---

66 König, Op. Cit Bruno Huber, *Conjunction.*

67 Sue Lewis, Op. Cit. *APWET*, page 33.

> and Wassily Kandinsky's *Concerning the Spiritual in Art* (1911), and observed colour tests developed by the Swiss psychotherapist Max Lüscher, in 1969. In Florence he started painting, producing an abstract every full Moon and one every new Moon. Although Bruno chose to focus on astrology in preference to art, and executed only one series of paintings, this engagement with the visual medium is demonstrated in the arrangement of the chart, showing the five levels fanning out from the central circle of the self, through the inner motivations represented by the aspect structure, to the driving planetary energies, outwards to the archetypal signs of the zodiac, and around the periphery are the mundane houses interacting with the environment. The chart is a mandala whose colours and shapes enable the astrologer to envisage the whole person whose chart is being read, so it is a truly esoteric space. Looking at the charts of Bruno and Louise, Bruno's might resemble a Himalayan mountain range, such as painted by the Theosophist Nicholas Roerich, with peaks and valleys, while Louise's opens out onto a broad plateau with tall poplars reaching for the heavens.

Roberto Assagioli

Louise describes the unique characteristics that made Roberto Assagioli such an effective mentor for the young couple during this period at the Institute[68].

> Roberto Assagioli was at the same time our friend, an affectionate father and helper. He resolved mental doubts, insecurities or conflicts on the highest, mental level. For me he was the archetypal wise man, he was unbelievably tolerant, benevolent and highly intelligent. You could never fool him, as he immediately saw through any veil of deception and tore it to shreds. That was his greatest quality. He solved all kinds of problems easily, suddenly they disappeared, were no longer troublesome or important; they were cleared up by his very presence. This healing influence also made him famous as a therapist. That is why so many people came to him after being failed by other psychologists or psychiatrists. He discovered the cause of their crises

68 Louise Huber, Op. Cit. *DAP*, page 17.

in their spiritual development and sorted things out by showing them the laws of the path of spiritual development.

His clarity of mind was invaluable for Bruno's astrological research. He could spot and immediately rectify any potential or hasty wrong conclusions of Bruno's research. This was naturally encouraging for us, and gave us the security to be more and more convinced of our cause. The knowledge that we had found something that would change the entire world of astrology motivated us to put all our energies into it. Assagioli often said that every young person who felt responsible for the world and its development had to construct his own area of responsibility, and that ours was the field of astrological psychology. We only felt ready for this great task after three years of training. With Roberto Assagioli's blessing, we then felt we had the courage – if not the means – to return to Switzerland and begin our risky but creative enterprise.

The rumour

Was this wise man simply facilitating the development of Bruno & Louise in a direction that aligned with his own professional and altruistic interests, or was there more to it than that?

Many have observed that there is a striking similarity in the physical features of Roberto and Bruno, and that there is a strikingly broad range of intelligence in each of these exceptional human beings. Also there were rumours of an affair between Roberto and Bruno's mother, Frau Anny Huber-Wuhrmann, both members of the Arcane School in Zürich. Could Roberto be Bruno's biological father? Although plausible, this is all rumour and speculation, albeit fuelled at times by both Bruno and Michael Huber.

Roberto Assagioli

Bruno, 1995

The truth of the matter is not known.

Roberto's blessing

Bruno & Louise did tell the story that, when they came to leave Florence, Roberto gave them each his blessing – specifically blessing Bruno's head and Louise's hands[69]. The wise Roberto understood their key strengths that would ensure success in their future 'area of responsibility'.

69 Verbal report from Richard Llewellyn on a conversation with Bruno & Louise.

6. Zürich and Founding of API

1962-1968

After the completion of their work with Assagioli, Bruno & Louise were ready to make their own way in life. They returned to Zürich.

A period of confusion

Bruno continues his story with a period of uncertainty and exploration of life options[71].

> At New Year 1962 we returned to Switzerland. Roberto Assagioli's textbook on *Psychosynthesis* was completed and our contract with the Psychosynthesis Institute of the U.S.A. came to an end. My Age Point was by now in the 6th house and had already entered the intercepted sign of Leo. Now what? That was the big question.
>
> Both Louise and I felt totally confused, as we didn't rightly know just what we wanted to do. On the one hand we had to cope with the stark reality of having to earn our daily bread, on the other hand we were still filled with the noble ideal of improving the lot of mankind. Added to this was the tantalising fact that I was really spoilt for choice. I had learnt a great deal during the past few years, and could have earned a living as an astrological or psychological counsellor, or perhaps as an artist? Or should I go back to photography or the cinema? Or... Or... I was torn in all directions.
>
> The conflict of the 6th house attacked me from all directions. We had been called to Geneva. We had been called to Florence. Now I had to find my own calling, that much I could see clearly. But how could I cope with a surfeit of abilities and possibilities which were very different from each other, not to say contradictory! Somehow I had to manage to bring them all under one hat, but this would have to be a huge field of interests, that didn't really exist in this world of ours.

71 Bruno Huber, Op.Cit. *DAP*, page 12.

And we also had to consider the social conditions of the time, and the actual jobs which might be available to me. But in the beginning I was most reluctant to abandon my hope of finding a job that would engage all my varied abilities.

That's how it came about that for the next six years I tried everything and anything that I could possibly do, and some things that I really couldn't do. These were the darkest years of my life, at least from the point of view of being successful and fulfilled, but at the same time the most fruitful and enlightening ones. I studied and worked very hard during this time, but my material success was minimal, I just learned over and over again to realise which jobs were not suitable for me.

Reporter and photographer with the boy scouts in the mountains.

The Neck of the Bottle

If only at that time I'd already understood the meaning of the Age Point in the 6th house I might have saved myself a lot of trial and error. But then perhaps I might not have learned such a lot about my own chart, and astrology in general. As for instance about intercepted signs[72] (Leo in my own chart), or about my Mars in this intercepted sign. This Mars dashed about wildly in a fierce attempt to achieve. Or about my Neptune in the following sign (Virgo) who tried to haul me already into his house, right across the intercepted Leo, by enticing me with his humanitarian ideals.

The Zürich Astrology Scene

On our return to Zürich in 1962, we once more got in touch with the astrological scene within the German speaking area. During our stay in Florence we neither saw nor heard anything astrological of

72 An intercepted sign is one that does not contain any house cusps. A planet in such a sign may have difficulty with expressing its energies, which may not be recognised by the world.

the slightest bit of interest to us, except of course Italian newspaper astrology, and also adverts by so-called astrologers, and soothsayers and magicians who extolled their prowess.

But even Switzerland couldn't really boast of an astrological scene. There were hardly any astrological books to be found, and those few that existed were hidden away in the farthest corners of a very small number of shops. One available book was a series written by Thomas Ring, called *Astrologische Menschenkunde*, the study of man from an astrological point of view, also a series of five volumes called *Astrologica* published by Metz, containing the Kundig ephemeris, which dominated the market for ephemerides for a long time. Reinhold Ebertin's *The Combination of Stellar Influences* featuring planetary midpoints was also available, and slowly more of his books. And the publishers Baumgartner continued to produce essays and manuscripts in somewhat haphazard fashion, a confusing collection of old and ancient methods of interpretation. There were just a few small groups of interested astrologers, but the groups were small, only locally known, and hard to find. Altogether there was no real corporate astrological body in Switzerland, and the only one in Germany was the K.A.A. (Cosmological Academy of Aalen) run by the Ebertin Dynasty. It warranted serious consideration because it attracted all

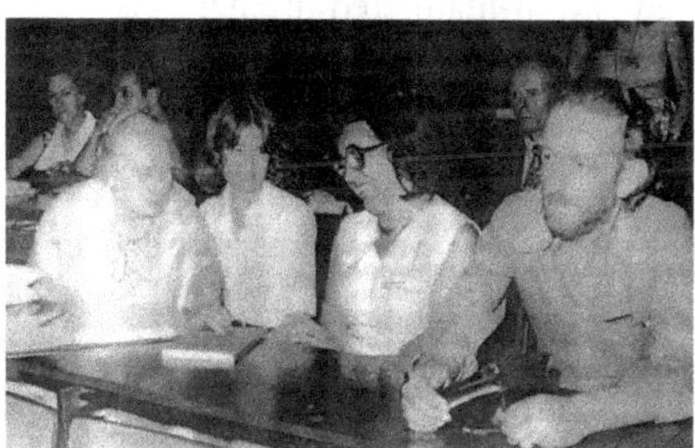

Bruno with Louise at a gathering in Aalen.
At far left is Mrs. von Ungern-Sternberg.

sorts of interesting people and they arranged regular and remarkable seminars. There were two other groups, both started after the war, which just about managed to exist, with sparse membership and few activities. They were the DAV (Company of German Astrologers), whose membership grew older and staler, and the Company of

Cosmobiosophists, which suffered a lot of infighting and thereby lost founder member Hans Genuit, and with him its impact and initiative. There was also the Hamburg School in northern Germany; in the inter-war years its founder Alfred Witte had written a book called *Regelwerk* (Book of Rules) which I came across by accident one day in an antique shop. Members of this group were at the congress in Aalen.

It was quite characteristic of this time, the sixties, that the various groups existed in isolation and disagreed on the best methods to use. Here is a typical example. One day, in the early sixties, Dr. Walter Koch was scheduled to give a lecture on his birthplace House System. Obviously I found this interesting as I was actually using this very method, and I knew Koch to be a learned author. So I looked forward to gaining interesting insights into the underlying mathematics of the system, and maybe an account of the development of his ideas. Louise and I went to his lecture full of joyful anticipation. For the first quarter of an hour Koch expounded the basics of his theory in rather convoluted language. But then the barracking began, one heckler accused him of plagiarism, which so upset Dr. Koch that he forgot what he'd planned to say and spent the next hour and a half in a confused attempt to defend himself, continually interrupted by ill-tempered and ill-mannered listeners. As a result we gained no information worth having. Finally we just left, very disappointed.

There were just a few exceptions to this dismal picture, for instance the rare seminars given by Thomas Ring. Mercifully, in contrast to his written work, his lectures were given in simple language and easy to follow. For me, his expositions and chart interpretations were the only fruitful and genuinely informative happenings of the astrological scene of that time.

Bruno's angina attack – 1964

During this period Bruno experienced an 'encounter with death' that proved a turning point[73].

My first encounter with death was in 1964. I had terrible angina that consigned me to bed with a fever of 40 degrees and suddenly I realized I couldn't breathe. With all my strength I stammered:

73 Bachmann, Op.Cit. Interview with Bruno Huber.

"Camphor, camphor…". Louise found camphor somewhere, put it to my nose, and then I recovered. It was a strange and very intense experience. I couldn't breathe and that was terrible. I thought I was going to die there and then, I saw myself lying dead.

That was one of the turning points of my life. From that moment onwards I began to work with astrology, that's to say, I stimulated Louise to write. You could say I moved things forward. This also took place at a Low Point – the one in house 6.

Louise's written horoscopes

Bruno thus stimulated Louise to return to offering written horoscope interpretations, as she describes[74]:

I began to offer written horoscopes in Adliswil near Zürich in 1964. After a while I was so busy with them that I was able to give up my part-time job, which had enabled us to keep our heads above water. In those years I did more than 1,000 written horoscopes. Unlike my first attempt in Stuttgart, I was now able to use the concept of astrological psychology, which gave me the security to know that I was not making mistakes and that I could provide better holistic and psychologically-viable readings. Thanks also to the knowledge I had acquired from the Arcane School, my esoteric horoscope readings were particularly well-received both at home and abroad.

A vocation realised

Bruno's story continues, as he realises what he should now devote his life to[75].

While helping friends astrologically, I learned in these years a great number of little rules of interpretation, as I came to call them, chiefly by means of the many friends, relatives and acquaintances who kept on coming to me with their problems and whose charts I studied. They told me the story of their lives, and asked for my advice. Needless to say, hardly any of them ever actually paid for our "invaluable services" (Louise and I had to take turns doing odd jobs to keep body and soul together) but our reward for this work came later and a different form.

---

74 Louise Huber, Op.Cit. *DAP*, page 17.
75 Bruno Huber, Op.Cit. *DAP*, page 12.

Through this "selfless" work of ours an increasing number of people became convinced of the quality and usefulness of such a serious pursuit of astrology. In the end this had far-reaching consequences. I had learned with a vengeance that I couldn't earn a decent living through psychology, that nobody wanted to buy my drawings and pictures [Bruno actually states elsewhere[76] that the best pictures he produced during this period were stolen during a house move, which he took as a signal that he was not after all destined to be an artist,] that photography and filming were too one-sided for me and that general jobbing required the acquisition of a wealth of subsidiary knowledge, such as pharmacology, music theory, how to build musical instruments, the history of art and culture. During all this time a group of people had collected around us who only wanted one thing from us: that we'd teach them the type of astrology which we practiced ourselves.

The penny didn't drop until 1967, when my AP had passed Neptune[77,78]. Yes, this would be our niche in the market place (sixth house theme), to become teachers of astrology.

At first I angrily rejected the very idea, it seemed far too narrow a field, a mere splinter out of my wealth of gifts. But then I suddenly realised that this was the bottleneck that had to be negotiated in the sixth house. Finally the decision to become teachers of astrology turned out to be the only financially viable venture, and it also proved to be the

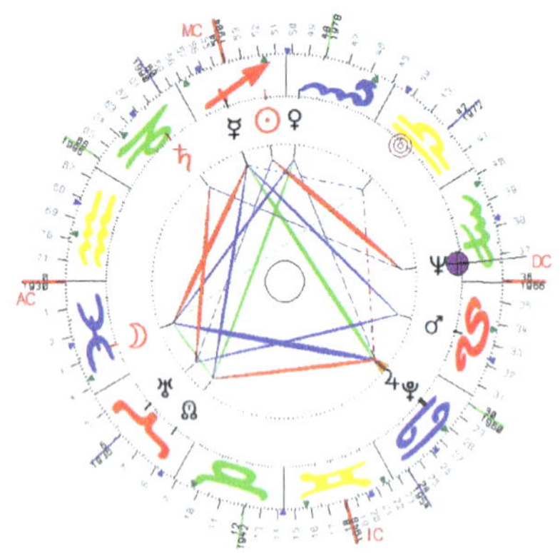

Bruno Huber
AP conjunct Neptune
September 1967

76 Bachmann, Op. Cit. Interview with Bruno Huber.

77 After passing through intercepted Leo, AP contacts Neptune and the visionary energy that sets Bruno on his main life task.

78 The story is told that this was particularly provoked by a man coming to the flat to buy a salon table and getting into conversation with Bruno about astrology, saying that he should teach it. Landolt, Bruno, "Zum 20. Todestag ven Bruno Huber", *Astrolog* 231, Oct 2019, page 12.

greatest endeavour I'd ever undertaken. And I can still say this with all my heart: I'd found my dream calling.

"Sir"

And so, towards the end of 1967, I began to compile a syllabus for teaching astrology. I certainly didn't find it easy, as there was no previous work to lean on. Any manuals I had so far seen seemed to me to be too dry, head oriented, and technological. After all, we were dealing with living material, with a science that revolved around living human beings. I had been told by a number of people of the difficulty they had learning astrology from books. They invariably didn't get very far and didn't enjoy it, as the books all emphasised the mathematics, the technicalities of setting up a chart, ad nauseam, whilst the interpretation was too abstract and academic. The word "incomprehensible" was mentioned over and again.

That's why I began, deliberately and systematically, to record my astrological know-how with the help of graphs and diagrams. A few tables listing meanings were unavoidable, also a few calculation tables. I approached my first few pupils with a mere 20 pages of teaching material in my hand, and my first few lectures consisted of explaining these pages to them, and illustrating their contents with examples drawn from real life. Then I took the merely symbolic interpretation of a specific detail and pointed it out in a chart with its various ramifications, enlarged on it, and compared it with the living reality of the life of the person concerned.

Louise for her part took on the organisation and administration involved. She bought a tiny advert in the local paper to inform the public about our intended lecture on astrology and sent invitations to our vast circle of friends and acquaintances. She hired a small hall in a restaurant, and we hoped fervently that a few outsiders might show an interest and attend the lecture, over and above those who had already told us of their interest in the subject.

Bruno gives talk
photo: family

We both remember vividly the fateful events of March 12th 1968. Off we went on our Lambretta, complete with overhead projector, and screen; it was pouring with rain, but we were determined to unleash our own private astrological revolution. About 30 people turned up at the *Karl dem Grossen* restaurant in Zürich. Oddly enough they were all strangers, only one turned up from the many who had actually asked us to give the talk.

Evidently the lecture turned out all right. It was my first public appearance, I can't remember for the life of me just what I actually said, but apparently the talk produced the desired affect. When, at the end of the lecture, we announced that we'd start a beginners' course next week, several people signed on there and then.

In all twenty people started the course the following week, we were able to teach them astrology, and still [1987] count some of them amongst our best friends. [Louise remarked[79]: "No one then imagined that this would be the start of a worldwide astrology movement."]

A few months later we started a parallel second course, that autumn we started a third one in Basel, and within the year teaching astrology was providing us with a decent living.

Organising Bruno

This wouldn't have happened without Louise's organisation. Here she describes how she decided that she needed to organise Bruno's life, which led to the founding of the *Astrologisch-Psychologisches Institut* (API)[80].

During this period Bruno and I had repeated crises, as we did not know exactly what Bruno should be working on. Although we were spiritually at one, we had a very different approach to everyday matters. Bruno was a very creative man, and painted beautiful pictures during this period. He didn't really care about existential issues, which was very often a strain for me. After a few arguments, I realised that his qualities were very different to mine, and I had no choice but to completely let go of my expectations and mistaken ideas. As I learned to use my organisational abilities to prepare a path that suited him, things finally started to improve for us. From that moment on, I took over responsibility, initially for organising Bruno's life, and then for the API Institute.

79 Louise Huber, ibid.

80 Louise Huber, Op.Cit. *DAP*, page 17.

7. Growth of API

1968-1991

Establishing an Institution

The events outlined at the end of the last chapter proved to be the start of a process leading to creation of the *Astrologish-Psychologisches Institut* (API) which, in 1968, had its first public lectures and courses.

Wolfhard König outlines the early stages[82].

> Very soon this evolved into a unique teaching course. It was systematically constructed, well ordered, well thought out, with excellent graphics which did justice to Bruno Huber the graphic artist (Moon-Jupiter/Pluto-Venus in a Large Talent triangle.) There was great emphasis on making everything easy to understand, with the aim of making astrological psychology a useful tool with which to tackle life's intricacies.
>
> Within a few years these courses could be found all over the German speaking area. Finally, in 1973, a 3-year teaching course was on offer with a Diploma at its conclusion. Therefore, what started as a revolutionary innovation (Uranus) born out of radical questioning of old methods, now began to clothe itself in a form and stability of its own (Saturn). Seen from an astrological perspective this surely constitutes a reconciliation of these two contradictory principles, which are square in Bruno Huber's chart.
>
> One of the purposes of the Diploma was to reassure any prospective client looking for help, that the astrologer had achieved a degree of technical competence. A knowledge of astrology was to be added to psychology, but at the same time the length and content of training was intended to be equal in value to that of other counselling professions – such as marriage guidance, child guidance and general counselling.

---

82 König, Op Cit. Huber, *Conjunction*, page 58.

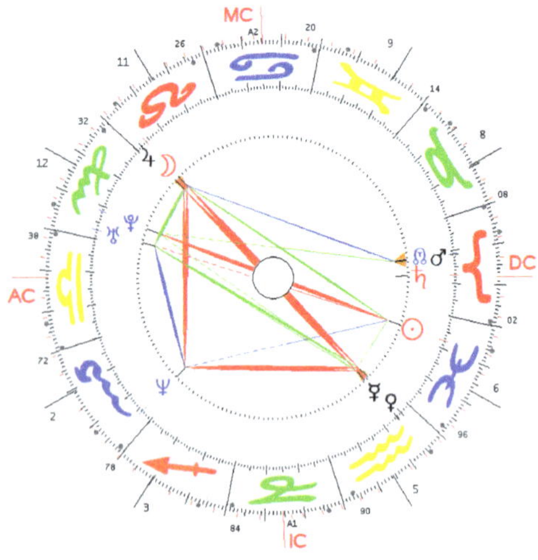

Formation of API Switzerland
12/03/1968, 20:08, Zürich, Switzerland

Louise later outlined the key periods of these early years, and related them to the chart for the formation of API[82]. These are summarised below[83].

Workshops and summer schools

The ongoing courses were soon supplemented by a range of workshops, summer schools and other regular events.

The first summer school, in Todtmoos-Rütte, was in July 1969, with the API AP opposite Mars/Node. In 1972 a series of workshops began for current students in Achberg which formed a mandatory part of the training and are ongoing to this day.

In 1977, when the API AP was passing over Neptune, the Hubers "managed to find two guest houses called Sardi and Mare in Pomonte on the west coast of the island of Elba[84]", where they held regular summer schools. Regular Ascension Day seminars also began in Morschach, Switzerland, and autumn seminars in Ötz, Tirol. 1977 also

82 This intriguing chart has unaspected Saturn in Aries, sitting on the DC – like Louise, controlling all that red working energy within.

83 Louise Huber, 'API Gründungshoroskop' (API Formation Chart), *Astrolog* 231, Oct/Nov 2019, pages 13-15.

84 Louise Huber, Op.Cit. *DAP,* page 17.

Summer School at Elba, 1984

saw establishment of a room in Zürich for Louise to hold monthly full moon meditations. That year also saw the birth of Bruno & Louise's first grandchild.

Mirjam Bertsch was closely involved in those early days of API. Her story on page 68[85] gives a feel for what those times were like for those involved.

Going global

Bruno became more widely known through being invited to speak at international conferences in Europe in 1974[86]. Such invitations became a regular feature of both of their lives.

In 1978 Bruno gave his first talk at a conference of the American Federation of Astrologers, which coincided with the passage of the API AP into the sign of Sagittarius. These evolved into biannual visits to USA, interspersed with talks given at the British Astrological Association conferences in England.

Louise, 1978

Bruno, date unknown

photos: family

85 Mirjam Bertsch, 'Abdankungsfeier Bruno Huber', *Astrolog* 113, Dec 99, page 2.

86 Mirjam Bertsch, ibid.

Mirjam Bertsch recalls the early days of API

On Monday 27 September 1971 I first attended a lecture by Bruno Huber. I was fascinated by the personable dynamic speaker who apparently described his new astro Method from three sides at the same time. Despite my skepticism I was immediately drawn in. The way was open through astrological psychology to a well-founded self-awareness. Now I had finally found the knowledge that I had been seeking for so long.

On Monday October 11th I began the first of 10 course evenings with Bruno and Louise at the round table in a back room of the then-in-need-of-renovation Karl der Crosse, in the old town of Zürich. Although I doubted in my diary whether I would ever understand such a wide area of astrology, I persevered. From January 1972 followed course on course. API Astrology had got under my skin.

At the same time there developed a deep empathy and friendship between Bruno, Louise and myself. I went to evening courses in St. Gallen and Basel, so that I was doing three parallel classes. For us aspiring young API students these were exciting pioneering days full of idealism. And there were parties in the Adliswil family apartment where we stuffed envelopes while discussing high flights of philosophy.

From 1972 the Zürich API courses took place in the bright rooms of the lyceum club and then in a related school. The number of participants rose rapidly. New course topics were frequently offered.

Beginning in 1972 the first Ascension Day seminar, in Achberg, had 28 participants and a range of exciting topics, including individuality and consciousness, Pluto and human development, esoteric astrology with Louise, determinism, fate and freedom. Thanks to Bruno's infectious enthusiasm we experienced true moments of inspiration and were aware of the limitless possibilities of psychological-spiritual development. These unforgettable experiences lasted and encouraged us for many years in the search for meaning. I am deeply grateful.

From the summer of 1973 I also visited seminars by Thomas Ring in Heilbronn. It was for me significant that I managed to bring together this founder of astrological human science and the 38 years younger Bruno Huber in Zürich, with a small circle of friends. A major topic was of course Moon/Saturn and the mother image. I exulted in the wise agreement of the two astro masters.

In 1974 Bruno was for the first time invited to speak at international congresses. As APl PR/secretary, I accompanied Bruno & Louise on long car trips to Germany, England, Milan. Bruno was driving his Ro-80 [a quirky German car] full of ideas and enjoyment of life.

Our first trip in September 1974 was to Paris to the ISAR Congress (International Society for Astrological Research.) There was the global network planned by the astrologers. In the evening we had much fun with Astro-games, which from then on were adopted in API workshops in Achberg, Elba, Morschach, Oetz. On the triumphal arch one (Etoile) with star-shaped roads leading off – twelve magnificent streets, Bruno imagined on that centre of Paris a giant horoscope with 12 parts, the Sorbonne University in the 9th house, the military school and Eiffel Tower in 8th House, the United Nations in the 7th house, and so on. Eyes, ears, all senses... Bruno was playful, fantasising, rhetorical...

Also to value was the input from father Reinhold Ebertin at the 27th cosmobiological meeting in Aalen (August 1975). Bruno's brilliant lecture on aspect-images suggested an echo in the mountains – which evoked whistles and boos from traditionalists, and frenetic applause from the open-minded. Ebertin was annoyed; but the old astrologer encouraged someone to speak to a young Huber colleague from Zurich: "Please, do anything you can to take astrology back into the universities." Bruno laughed – a hearty laugh...

Unforgettable is also the holiday week with Bruno, Louise and Uschi Hunkeler at end of Aug. 1975 in Elba. How vividly Bruno described stories of the ancient world, inspired by the Etruscan antiques – whose thinking is directly related to life. There emerged here the idea to hold seminars on Elba.

In June 1977 a group went by bus from Zürich to Pomonte, staying overnight in Florence. The highpoint was Bruno's city tour on the Sunday morning. Since his study years with Prof. Dr. Assagioli he knew Florence well with all its beautiful sights. It was for us an exquisite experience.

World Astrology Congress

World Astrology Congress 1981

Inspired by this American experience, Bruno & Louise wanted to establish a similar event in Europe. They got together with like-minded astrologers Claude Weiss and Ueli Sauter to establish the first World Astrology Congress in Zürich in 1981. This was very successful and became a biannual event.

Astrolog magazine

Bruno had long desired for there to be a magazine of astrological psychology. After several false starts, the magazine *Astrolog* had its first issue in April 1981[87], aligned with that first World Astrology Congress[88]. Louise was not sure if it would work out, but the first issue sold over 1000 copies[89]. *Astrolog* became the regular magazine of astrological psychology, coming out every 2 months, with Bruno as chief editor and Rita Keller handling layout and practical issues.

The API Centre, Adliswil

In 1983 the Hubers purchased the API House or API Centre in Obertilistrasse in the village of Adliswil, just outside Zürich. As well as being their home, this centre became the focus for API, their work with students, consultations, chart technology, production of *Astrolog* and other activities[90].

API is now well established

Shortly after moving into the API Centre, the API AP moved into the sign Capricorn, appropriately corresponding with the fact that API was now well established and internationally respected.

API logo

---

87 Louise Huber, 'Wie es begann: Die ersten Nummern vom Astrolog', *Astrolog* 166, Nov 2008, page 8..

88 Wolfhard König, 'Der Astrolog', *Astrolog* 166, Nov 2008, page 16.

89 Landolt, Bruno, 'Rückblick auf eine Erfolgsgeschichte', *Astrolog* 200, Aug 2014, page 22.

90 The API Centre is described on page 137.

Distance learning

In 1986 Louise arranged for the new distance learning (correspondence) course of the English Huber School to be translated into German and adopted by API as one of its offerings. Elke Gut was one of the team running this, and eventually became its lead[91].

Ethical and professional

The Huber approach to astrology and psychology from the beginning had a strict ethical basis, reflecting their philosophy outlined in the introduction to their book *Life Clock*[92]:

> It is obvious that a more aware life brings greater freedom as well as greater responsibility. By gaining a greater influence on the environment and upon events, personal responsibility grows accordingly. We can say that free will develops in direct proportion to how ready we are to use our abilities, our interests, and goals in the service of the whole evolution of the personality.
>
> Our development depends essentially upon motivation. A healthy will can only be directed toward the good, toward growth and value development. This motivation is dependent upon individual ethical development. The capacity for self-determination, the ability to choose among different possibilities and even act against one's own vital needs and interests for the good of the whole, leads to a cleansing of motives and to the development of a spiritually oriented personality.

This was reflected in the API code that all students were required to sign. In 1989 the separate organisation (from API) API International was formed, with Bruno as its first president, with the aim of providing a basis for a professional approach to astrological psychology to be taken internationally[93]. The Hubers' ethical code was adopted by Huber schools everywhere. Because of its importance we spell out the version adopted by the English Huber School on page 72.

---

91 Louise Huber, 'Der Werdegang des API', *Astrolog* 103, Apr 1998, page 6. Also personal contribution by Elke Gut Oct 2020.

92 Bruno & Louise Huber, *LifeClock The Huber Method of Timing in the Horoscope*, HopeWell, 2006, page 14.

93 Wolfhard König, '20 Jahre - API International', *Astrolog* 162, Mar 2008, page 2.

The API Code - as adopted by English Huber School

Basic Attitude

1. We identify with the general declaration of human rights: "All human beings are to be allowed equal rights and liberties, are born equal in rights and dignity, are endowed with reason and conscience and should meet each other in the spirit of brotherhood ..."

2. We regard astrology exclusively as a diagnostic tool, with which we can recognise differences in character, problems of the human psyche and of psychological-spiritual development. Thus, astrological knowledge should above all be used to gain self-knowledge and as therapeutic help, as well as a means for solving conflicts – and not for prediction of the future.

3. Astrological psychology combines the astrological knowledge of the past with modern psychological insights. It is capable of explaining a person[1]s subjective attitude and its cause by revealing his inherent motivations and the conditioning affecting them. An astrological-psychological counsellor or teacher must have solid psychological knowledge in order to be able to fully grasp the problems of another person.

4. The basic concept of astrological psychology is based on the understanding of man as a whole; he has a psyche which is linked with the environment, but he is also a spiritual entity (individuality) who can be responsible for itself. With this basic concept it is impossible to consider or treat man as predetermined or like a computer.

5. We take as a precept the originality of the human individual and therefore regards uniform thinking only valid within the context of the subjective, single being. A person can only be understood in his individual character and manner and the corresponding subjective standards.

Research

6. It is our open policy to support only those astrological research results and methods, which can be proved by the reality of the human situation.

7. Research should bring proof for traditional knowledge, or it should develop new systems of classification and methodical practices which are empirically repeatable in the therapeutic situation. The astrological-

psychological counsellor/ teacher should constantly cultivate an attitude of a researcher.

8. Astrological research must work out its own humane-scientific methods of proof. We refuse to proceed along the lines of the contemporary system rule of the natural sciences. Statistics is only a conditionally suitable means for understanding the individuality and complexity of man.

Determination and Adaptation

9. The changeability of collective norms is historically evident. Any application of temporary or local collective norms for the purpose of assimilation into the community (adaptation) implies the restriction of a free and full maturing process. Thus, adaptation cannot and must not be the motivating expectation of the astrological psychologist. This applies especially to indoctrination, discipline, behavioural therapy and reflex training.

10. Like many modern schools of psychology, the astrology of the past has been geared toward behavioural determination. Any statement made along those lines inhibits the freedom of thought and action, because it pushes a person into a defensive attitude and self-fulfilling prophecies. Astrological psychology is not fortune-telling but a particularly apt psychological diagnostic tool. Therefore, to make concrete predictions for the future has to be considered unscrupulous.

11. As of now, astrology is not able to explain the astrological cause and effect mechanism in natural-scientific terms. Astrology is, however, able to use this mechanism perfectly in the form of the individual horoscope, when the astrologer regards it pragmatically as an indicating device for human character. The Goal: Freedom and Responsibility for Oneself.

12. The synthesis of psychology and astrology makes possible both a differentiated understanding of personality, and an integration and restructuring of the whole person. The creative energies of the personality are liberated and the person, taking initiative and responsibility for himself, begins to rearrange and restructure his life.

The only acceptable goal of the astrological-psychological counsellor and teacher must be to increase the freedom of the person who is being counselled.

A Complementary Relationship

How did it all work, and what was the contribution of each of Bruno & Louise to the success of the enterprise?

Louise – The organising force

Louise 1998

Louise was undoubtedly the formidable organising force behind the API enterprise that eventually trained thousands of students. A look at her chart shows a strong second house Taurean Sun pinning an incomplete Trapeze figure which dominates the chart. People with this aspect figure are usually "dominant within a group, where they serve as a role model..."[94] Louise made things happen.[95]

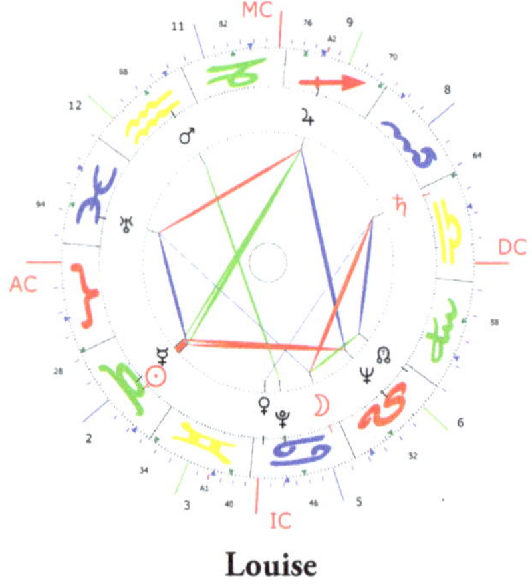

Louise

94 Joyce Hopewell, *Aspect Patterns in Colour*, HopeWell, 2010, page. 46.

95 Text from article by Barry Hopewell, 'The Hubers and their Legacy', *Astrological Journal* 2017.

Louise gave more insight into her character and the relationship with Bruno in the following reflections at age 79[96]:

Taurus

I am a Taurean woman, nearly a double Taurus with Sun on the cusp of house 2. By that I mean I am a strong and stable person, who engages completely with my ideals, and when I conceive of something important I carry it through to its conclusion. I have a great capacity for overcoming difficulties and attacks.

Obstacles stimulate me in a special way, because I want to overcome them. I will take considerable risks to plumb the depths of a task and actualize what I care about.

Pluto

The Pluto/Mars quincunx in my chart, disconnected from the rest of the aspect structure, has a particularly masculine strength. This aspect also signifies that when I am convinced of something, nobody can make me change my mind however hard they try. Whereas we might generally speak of the stubbornness of Taurus, really this refers to the ability to persevere with a task without deviating from it. The Pluto/Mars aspect gives me the necessary motivation to achieve this.

Pluto is for me a planet of evolution. Evolution is the all-embracing goal, the ultimate path to which I am committed in all I do. Things should be in harmony with the Whole, to me there is no alternative.

Balancing will and sensitivity

I have learnt to protect myself because I have suffered wounds, above all in love and relationships. During the war, when AP was on Pluto (October 1944) the person I loved died. Later, in prison, I experienced an unhappy relationship. Death has always been present and the theme of separation has always been distressing to my Moon in Cancer and Sun in Taurus.

The vulnerability remains. Probably this lunar sensibility is a necessary component of my psychic development that prevents me from being excessively strong and hard. If I were only this strong and masculine woman I would be too one-sided. It's the equilibrium of yin and yang. When I accept both parts as fundamental to my essence, I can live well.

---

96 Verena Bachmann, 'Interview with Louise Huber', *Conjunction* 65, page 13 on.

Renunciation

My Moon and Venus in Cancer, on the individualization axis 4/10, struggle with the impossible process of individuation resting on total surrender and absolute monogamy. I need to get love for myself. Symbolically, I need to learn how to nourish myself without expecting someone else to feed me. And this has been my process. Once learnt, the Capricornian part integrates itself. This has been my goal, that's to say my appointed destiny: that I should aspire to independence. Being married to a person like Bruno brought me this, because Bruno was a person very motivated by freedom.

It was a great opportunity for self-development. Whenever, with Saturn on LP7, I demanded something of Bruno, I never got it. On many occasions, I felt as if I was crying out in the desert. When I remonstrated or accused him of something, or wanted to make him feel guilty, he simply did not react. He never engaged with any kind of blackmail nor was he moved by feelings of guilt. With Bruno, none of this worked.

This conflict did not separate us because our eyes were fixed on something higher. The little crises invariably gave way to the great objective and the grand vision: to build API.

It was not easy, but it only affected the little game of partnership. A 7th house Saturn like mine demands, makes recriminations, wants to set boundaries, and seeks security and confirmation. I tried to play this little game with Bruno but he did not respond. I had no choice but to conquer it internally, by renunciation and transformation.

Now that I am nearly 80 years old, when I look back I have to say: "it was painful but appropriate". This has enabled me to accomplish parts of my lifelong task that would otherwise have remained incomplete.

The esoteric foundation

I persisted because of my esoteric work. Through the Arcane School and the work of Alice Bailey I became aware that I had a task, and through my meditations I knew that I must meet my goal at a higher level. The seed thought for Taurus is: "I see, and when the Eye is opened, all is illumined." This enabled me always to see the positive side and the potential for development, whatever happened.

First astrology courses

At the beginning we only had five to ten students. Then I had the idea of organizing larger groups that were more financially rewarding. In this way I began to use my organisational skills and took the reins. During the war I had learnt that anyone who is not capable of organizing becomes a victim. And I was no victim. My instinct for self-preservation had been well exercised and was in my favour.

Complementary

Bruno and I complemented each other very well but it took some time because our personalities were polarized. With such opposing characters, it was never easy. Spiritually we were united, but in daily activities we were polar opposites.

We had to go through a learning process to resolve this conflict. At first I thought (this was what I had heard from other people) that I must abandon the maternal role I had adopted with Bruno, and that he must be left to do things on his own. But when I took this attitude, everything went badly. We had many discussions about it.

For ten years we had our ups and downs: I said white and he said black. It was not easy to learn to use our polarity in a creative way. I used to think that at the material level Bruno needed to function in an intelligent way, as I did, but this didn't work: he was a completely different type of person from me. During one very productive interchange he said: "You have never done anything for me." This upset me badly. I had done so many things for him, and now he said that! Suddenly the blindfold fell from my eyes: instead of reproaching him constantly with my Saturn when this achieved nothing, I could organize for him.

That was in 1964 [Louise's AP had just passed over Saturn.] I was also very radical. As far as organization was concerned, I never expected anything of him. I let him do all the creative work. Once I dedicated myself to this role, API started to grow (before then we always lived a hand-to-mouth existence.)

Bruno – The researcher

Bruno photo Harald Zittlau

The astrological-psychological creative input to the API enterprise undoubtedly came from Bruno. He did the research, spotted the patterns, produced and tested the theories. How did he see himself[97]?

> First and foremost, I am a psychologist and that's of key importance to me. Stated simply, I work with people as a psychologist trying to help them lead better lives. I see the horoscope as a diagnostic tool to consider and explore from the psychological point of view.
>
> For me it's about the level of consciousness I continually face up to. I want to understand the world, I want to understand it better each time, and it's damnably big and complicated. There's always something new I haven't yet seen or understood, whether it's about the human being or the cosmos. For me the human being and his world is fully analogous with the cosmos, not only in the astrological sense but also in itself.
>
> I don't want to appear like a philosopher. I've read too many repugnant philosophies. I wouldn't call myself a philosopher for all the world. But evidently, I also philosophize… searching for meaning. Everything should make sense if it concerns the human being because, if it doesn't make sense, the human being doesn't feel happy. I manage my mystical side, the part that comes from the sign of Pisces, as scientifically as I can.

97 Bachmann, Op.Cit. Bruno interview.

Bruno's perspective on the relationship

Just before he died, Bruno reflected on their relationship together[98].

> We are still together. But this is because we had a common spiritual base from the beginning. For this you need someone with a similar thought structure, not necessarily the same dogmas but there needs to be a common language, and this worked for us. We were both interested in astrology. We've always known where we were heading, we've always been aiming for the same goal. And this has been the putty that binds us, our alignment. We wanted to do something that would serve human development while also supporting ourselves… Evidently, on the psychic level we have had our ups and downs. But if the spiritual plane is clear, the rest doesn't matter much.
>
> We are absolutely complementary, like two poles, better described as two worlds. In terms of character and opinion conditioned by the environment we're polar opposites, even in the details. For example, if Louise has a stomach ache she takes a pill. But, if I am the one with the stomach ache and I take the same pill it has no effect. I have to do the opposite… or something like that. This complementarity achieves good results. In our work for the school we complement each other in a fabulous way. We've never had competitive struggles.
>
> Problems didn't arise because we're fundamentally different. What one doesn't know how to do the other can do very well and vice-versa. We never have squabbles. There have been moments when I've taken decisions because Louise either did not want to or could not, but we have always pulled through together.

98 Bachmann, Op.Cit. Bruno interview.

Bruno and Technology

When Bruno began his astrological explorations all charts were hand-drawn and most were in black-and-white. During his early explorations he became convinced that colour was the way to make a meaningful chart. When his new-style chart was first shown to the world it was all done with coloured pens on a pre-printed chart form or acetate.

The inkjet printers we take for granted today did not begin to appear until the late 1970s. Before that, expensive graph plotters were used to create some astrological charts. With his strong aesthetic sense, Bruno was always trying to use the best equipment he could to create his charts. Of course, this required that appropriate chart software be developed. So Bruno worked with software developers to produce the right software for Huber charts.

Bruno's standards were high, the charts had to conform to certain standards before they were approved for use by API students – quality of graphics, colours and width of aspect lines, Koch houses, Huber orbs, marking of Low and Balance Points, and so on. For example, in 1992 he reported in an article on three programs then available: Astro-Plus, AstroVisa and Astrosys[99]. That same year there appears an advert for a chart and data service Computer Cortex[100]. Many students would have used such a service rather than grapple with their own software. A Cortex was later installed in the API Centre.

In 1995 Bruno Landolt became Swiss representative for AstroVisa. Eventually this program became unmaintainable and he became aware of a new program developed by Juan Saba in Argentina. The result of their subsequent collaboration was the program MegaStar[101], which became the program of choice for many students and practitioners. For Juan Saba's story see page 132.

Bruno was an early enthusiast for emerging networked technology. Your editors recall a visit to the API Centre in 1997 when the house was seamlessly networked between several computers, between Bruno's office up on high and the *Astrolog* workshop down in the basement.

---

99 Bruno Huber, 'Software', *Astrolog* 69, August 1992, page 10.

100 Advertisement Computer Cortex, *Astrolog* 71, December 1992, inside cover,

101 'Astrologiesoftware, Computer und Drucker: Interview mit Bruno Landolt', *Astrolog* 129, Aug 2002, page 25.

The First Huber Books

The Huber teachings were initially given out in talks, seminars, courses and workshops, but eventually became codified into a series of publications. In 1974, Bruno & Louise founded their own publishing company *API Verlag* to publish their own books in German.

Man and His World / The Astrological Houses

In 1975, their first book *Man and His World*[102] was published, first of a planned series on the newly coined *astrological psychology*, introducing their work to a wider circle than those directly influenced by their talks, workshops and seminars. It outlined their approach to the psychological significance of the horoscope and each of its five levels, focusing on the psychological significance of the astrological houses and the various zones and polarities in the chart.

1975 Man and His World

This was astrologically revolutionary at the time, including as it did the Dynamic Energy Curve of energy in the houses and its psychological implications. Astrologer Noel Tyl's introduction welcomed it thus[103]:

> Bruno and Louise Huber study the astrological houses in adamantly practical terms. They group concerns within the human condition into dynamically functional units of understanding. Their fresh psychodynamic insights place man into his world armed with richly textured understanding and individualistically creative remedial options. The Hubers' penetrating study of man and his world uses astrology to delineate a way of life within the present. Life ceases to be a cause to be avoided. Life becomes a stimulus we can affect.
>
> This book is essential. It is the freshest and most penetrating view of the houses I have seen in the astrological literature. Its title could easily have been *You and Your World*, so engagingly personal is its psychodynamic style. It guides us another big step forward to what we astrologers espouse but easily forget: that life is to be lived in

---

102 Bruno & Louise Huber, *The Astrological Houses: A Psychological View of Ourselves and Our World (Houses)*, HopeWell 2011. First pub German 1975 as *Der Mensch und seine Welt* (*Man and His World*), tr English Haloli Richter, pub Samuel Weiser 1978.

103 Huber, Op Cit. *Houses*, page *viii*.

terms of creative negotiation; that, to a great degree, it is what we make it; and that miracles emerge only when we know our positions – and our gods' – upon the battlefield.

We owe much gratitude to the Hubers for sharing their part of the world of astrology that surrounds us all.

A New Science of Man

We can feel the ambition of Bruno & Louise at that time in their introductory notes[104]:

> We feel close to a 'new science of man,' wherein modern psychological perception and ancient astrological wisdom are blended.
>
> In this book we introduce the astrological house system in its original natural state and transform it into a modern psychological thought form. From the house system, we deduce the basic behavioural psychological attitudes of mankind, how we react to our environment and how the environment then reacts to us.
>
> The system of analysis we present proportions and refines psychological diagnosis and shifts mankind away from numbers and mathematical formulae into the centre of life and cosmic occurrences. We teach a psychologically differentiated analysis that recognizes people in their true nature. An evaluation like 'good' or 'bad' is avoided on principle: we respect people's individuality and view them holistically. The synthesis of psychology and astrology affords a differentiated grasp of the personality as well as an integration and reshaping of the whole human being. This gives opportunity for the development of creative potentials.
>
> We share with you the great depth and diversification of the twelve houses, or life areas, as a reference system to the real world as well as to psychological processes, those that constantly occur between mankind and each individual environment. We are all striving for a better understanding of astrology, of ourselves, and our relationship to the environment.

Man and His World / The Astrological Houses proved the Hubers' all-time best seller, with lifetime sales of the Weiser English edition alone at over 16,500 copies.

---

104 Huber, Op Cit. *Houses*, page *ix*.

Life Clock

In 1980 and 1983 came two volumes on Age Progression[105] describing another of Bruno's major innovations, showing how the natal chart can be used as a *Life Clock* identifying key psychological influences at different times in life. The introduction contains this concise summary[106].

> Age progression is a relatively new concept. Through long years of research and twenty years of counselling and teaching, we have developed and successfully applied this system. It is not a hypothesis; the method has been used by many psychologists and astrologers in their practices. It is a kind of time mechanism within the horoscope, an individual life clock. This clock can indicate where we are in life and how we can make the best of current influences in the light of problems past, present, or future. Age progression refers to psychological processes, not to outer events.

Age progression has proved a valuable diagnostic tool in counselling and self understanding.

Astrological Psychosynthesis

During those same years of the early 1980s *API Verlag* published three smaller volumes by Bruno, on *Intelligence in the Horoscope* (1981), *Love and Relationship in the Horoscope* (1981), and *Personality and Integration* (1984). These notably introduced the holistic approach to chart interpretation, the role of planets in intelligence and relationship, how challenges of personality integration can be related to the positions of the particular personality (ego) planets in the chart and their links with each other, and introduced the concept of the Family Model, which highlights relationships between mother, father and child. This information did not appear in English until 1991, when a combined edition was published under the title *Astrological Psychosynthesis*[107].

---

105 Bruno & Louise Huber, *LifeClock The Huber Method of Timing in the Horoscope*, HopeWell, 2006. First pub in German 1980, 1983 in two volumes *Life Clock I and II.* tr. English by Haloli Richter and Transcript Ltd., pub Samuel Weiser, 1982,86.

106 Huber, Op Cit. *LifeClock*, page 4.

107 Bruno Huber, *Astrological Psychosynthesis*, HopeWell 2006. First pub German in 3 vols 1981-84. Tr English Agnes Shellens, pub Aquarian Press 1991, Samuel Weiser 1996.

Intuitive approach

A key part of this holistic approach to chart interpretation was the intuitive consideration of the pattern of the aspects in the chart[108].

> Viewed in its entirety the aspect structure is a symbolic representation of our consciousness, formed by the life energies available to us. That's why it is possible to 'see' the inner motivation inherent in a chart only by using our senses, by means of a meditative approach. We aim to let the visual impression speak to us as it is created within us when we contemplate the whole image. We have to cultivate our ability to think and 'feel ourselves into' the picture, and must learn to work with our powers of empathy and perception, not using the analytical, mercurial mind, but by relying on the jupiterian function of sensing, visualizing and opening our inner awareness. In this way we may just be able to intuit the quintessence of the person concerned in visual form. After all, the aspect structure is a symbol, a mandala, which has an energy of its own, with the facility to speak to our intuition.

The Amphora – piercing the Eggshell

This book also introduces Bruno's 'Amphora' model of the human psyche (page 85), which is an astrological-psychological-spiritual development of Roberto Assagioli's well-established 'Egg' model of the psyche used in psychosynthesis (page 2). The planets are all placed at the relevant level of the model[109].

As you can see, the Egg has been opened out at the top, to the world of spirit. At the neck of the amphora lies Neptune, planet of universal love – the only way out for the ego.

Where the top of Assagioli's egg was lies Uranus, planet of astrology, research and new structures. It is the job of Uranus to *pierce the eggshell* and to break through the top of the egg, the shell of the ego. Bruno called Uranus[110] *the egg piercer*, using the analogy of piercing through an egg shell, much as a baby chick does when it hatches. The mind is the piercing, searching arrow, just like the continental glyph for Uranus ⛢, breaking out of the confines of the egg.

---

108 Bruno Huber, Op.Cit. *Astrological Psychosynthesis*, page 24.

109 Bruno's version of the Amphora includes continental symbols for Uranus ⛢, and for Pluto ♇.

110 Joyce Hopewell's notes from Froebel College, June 1992.

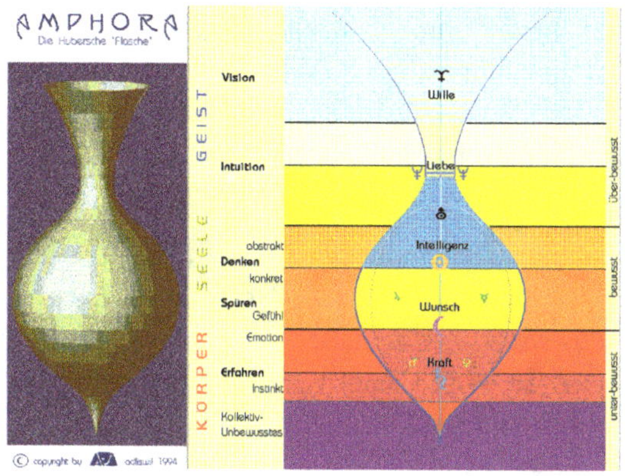

Bruno's Amphora
Bruno's own illustration

The shell represents the mental arguments we have to protect us but the impetus to break out comes from within as our spirituality is awakened. When this happens we leave the realms of normal consciousness and reach for answers "out there" beyond our normal range. It means taking risks, but it's a movement of mind and consciousness.

Reflections and Meditations

Throughout her life Louise remained a dedicated student of the perennial wisdom and the work of Alice Bailey, holding monthly full moon meditation meetings with students and others interested. As part of this process, she wrote her own book of meditations on the Signs of the Zodiac[111], based on this experience, providing a valuable resource to astrologers and meditators. This was published in 1981.

Spiritual development

Over the next decade the Hubers' ideas on spiritual development and transformation gradually emerged. *Life Clock III* was published in German in 1985, and in English by Samuel Weiser in 1991 under the title *Astrology and the Spiritual Path*. This covered a number of factors related to spiritual development, including the concept of stress planets that can drain energy from other parts of the psyche, the spiritual

111 Louise Huber, *Reflections and Meditations on the Signs of the Zodiac*, American Federation of Astrologers, 1984. First published in German, API Verlag 1981.

significance of Low Points, and the House Chart which indicates environmental demands on the individual.

Moon Node Astrology

Moon Node Astrology: The Inner Compass of Evolution[112] was published in German in 1991. The moon nodes can give important indicators for spiritual development, and the Moon Node Chart gives information on the unconscious shadow personality (karma from another viewpoint). With the House Chart this leads to working with the three charts, as anticipated by Alice Bailey: "Astrologers will eventually find it necessary to cast three horoscopes..."[113]

This is perhaps less accessible than the other Huber works, but they were quite convinced of its value, exemplified by these words from the introduction[114]:

> During many years of teaching and consultancy work, we have been told by numerous students how fruitful they have found an understanding of the Nodes and of the Moon Node Chart. They were able to accept themselves for what they were, and could quickly deepen consciousness. Those with esoteric leanings recognise the roots of their problems in former lives; and many things in their present lives that they had been unable to accept made sense at last, being seen as part of a greater whole. They confirmed that... striking expansions of consciousness, transformations and processes of self development were unleashed, and that these were much more profound than mere character analysis of personality traits.

The first five books – latest English versions: Houses, Life Clock, Astrological Psychosynthesis, Reflections & Meditations, Moon Node

112 Bruno & Louise Huber, *Moon Node Astrology: The Inner Compass of Evolution*, HopeWell 2005. First published in German in 1991.

113 Alice Bailey, *A Treatise on White Magic*, Lucis Press, 1934, p. 439.

114 Huber, Op Cit. *Moon Node*, page *xvi*.

Whirlwind of Activity

API was a major operation, with Bruno & Louise at the centre making everything happen. Louise summarises how API took over their lives in a whirl of teaching, travelling, research, writing, organising,...[115]

> We have been constantly busy from the moment API began. In 36 years, we have never had a moment to stop, rest or look back; things have always been moving forwards, growing and working towards the future. Again and again we have had to innovate in order to keep going.
>
> The creative impetus came mainly from Bruno, and later also from our son Michael. Together they used their indefatigable spirit of research to develop the whole concept of the Huber Method, which has given so much to so many people.
>
> However, our pioneering spirit has met with resistance from traditional astrology. Our innovations even made us enemies, which had to be dealt with. This also stimulated our spiritual growth, though. We often had to leave our personal wishes unsatisfied and transcend ourselves, in order to be able to work on our transpersonal mission and remain inwardly open. This motivation gave us much strength and support. In hindsight, we could say that the pioneering days were very good times that we would not have missed for the world.
>
> Until 1991 we were travelling nearly every weekend and held courses in many German cities including Hanover, Hamburg, Berlin, Cologne and Bonn. We were active throughout the year in Munich and Stuttgart and of course in the Swiss cities of Zürich, Basel, Bern, Lucerne, Winterthur and St. Gallen.
>
> In the 1980s and 1990s, we also participated in many conferences in the USA, England, France, Denmark, Brazil, Russia, the Czech Republic and Hungary. Our teaching activities thus expanded into other countries, and we gained international acceptance.

115 Louise Huber, Op. Cit. *DAP*, page 17.

Louise related this constant activity to the red-green dominance in the chart of API Switzerland and the Irritation Rectangle figure containing the crossed red opposition aspects[116]. She also pointed to the Piscean Sun on the Balance Point of the 6th house as reflecting their ongoing attitude that they were performing a service to humanity; the opposition to Pluto gave the energy and perseverance that was necessary[117].

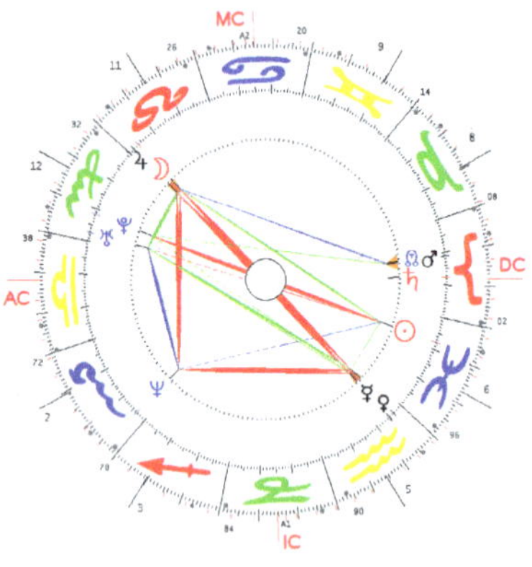

API Switzerland

A new dawn?

By 1989, with thousands of students and international recognition spreading to countries across the world, as the API AP passed into Aquarius, it really did seem that a new age of astrological psychology was dawning, spearheaded by Bruno & Louise Huber.

116 Louise Huber, 'Der Werdegang des API', *Astrolog* 103, Apr 1998, page 4.
117 Louise Huber, ibid.

Bruno is Forced to Slow Down

Bruno was fully involved in the whirlwind of activity until he suffered a heart attack in 1991. Here he reflects on that process and the relationship with his chart[118].

In my chart, I have Neptune on a major cusp on the DC, 4-5 degrees above. Up to the age of about sixty I followed a rule, a formulation of love that came from my mother. I have a trine from Saturn in the eleventh house in Capricorn to that Neptune which shows it clearly comes from the mother. My mother said "You must always be good to people. If you do good to people they will be good as well." She made me take that profession, and made me work around the clock in doing so. Until I got a heart attack.

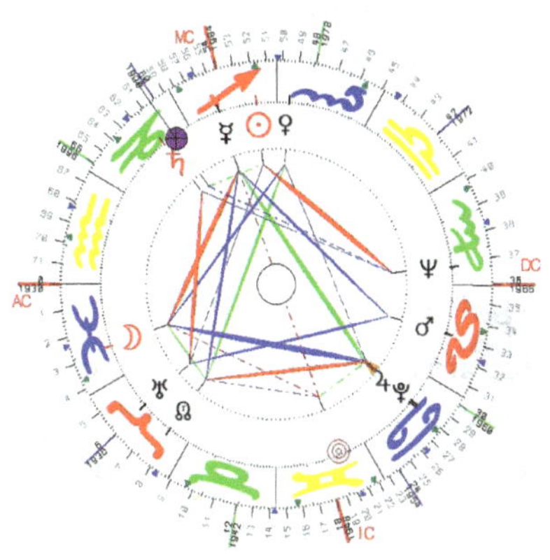

Bruno's chart showing AP trine Neptune
22 March 1991

At the age of sixty one I had a heart attack – because I had done too much, because I couldn't say "No, now it's enough, stop!" When people came and asked questions, demanded something, wanted help, etc. I would work around the clock. Nobody can do that really. So until the age of sixty I didn't realise that I had this fixation, then suddenly I could clearly denominate it, could see it. It came from my mother, she worked and lived that way.

She was a hairdresser, had a little business, and worked with people like that. Somebody could come at 9.30 in the evening and my mother would say "Oh, you have a headache, come in", and the person would go away without a headache. Fine, great. But, one day a policeman stood there and said "You're working at the wrong time – no good." She was told this way, I was told by a harder way. I did it much longer. Can you see what I mean, as an instance?

---

118 Bruno & Louise Huber, *Astrology and the Seven Rays*, HopeWell, 2006.

> It's tricky with Neptune. It's even more tricky with Pluto because the feeling of greatness overshadows even more your rational thinking, your proportional thinking.

In his late interview Bruno came back to that link with Neptune[119]:

> I had my heart attack when my age point made a trine to Neptune. I had hoped that something like that might have been linked to the powerful influence of Saturn but it happened a little earlier[120], at the exact moment of the trine with Neptune. That revealed to me a neglected dimension that needed attention. In this sense, it's significant that Neptune and Moon are in opposing signs.

Aggression and sensitivity

Towards the end of his life, under perceptive questioning, Bruno reflected on his own relationship with impulses towards aggression and sensitivity reflected in his own chart[121].

> Aggression and imposition as ends in themselves don't exist for me. But when it's a matter of maintaining a spiritual principle, I will defend it on any turf. And I have enormous resistance! Instead of violence and aggression, I possess great powers of endurance. Mars is on a low point, and intercepted, with blue aspects…
>
> I've never allowed myself to be aggressive. Sometimes I've had moments of rage, but I could never allow myself to behave aggressively so as to score points. My ethics wouldn't allow it. That's why I couldn't take up contemporary astrology without founding my own school so that I could use my own method. That meant I didn't have to discuss with others who was right. In the beginning, I was challenged quite a few times and maddened when, following some objection, the person in question didn't give a clear answer but instead quoted from a book. So I decided to go my own way. For me, that provided a solution that prevented me from becoming aggressive. I applied my energy to being there, persisting. My motto has always been to stay in there and persevere, irrespective of whatever reactions might arise.

---

119 Bachmann, Op.Cit. Bruno Huber interview.

120 AP conjunction with Saturn in April 1992 comes just over 1 year after the AP trine Neptune.

121 Bachmann, Op.Cit. Bruno Huber interview.

Sensitivity – Neptune/Pisces emphasis

We've already seen that Bruno had a very sensitive nature from childhood. How did he cope with the demands of API? Vital for Bruno was the inclusion in the API Centre of his very own place for retreat, as he explained[122]:

> In the API house I have my study and on the floor above I have my room and a little kitchen, so that when I need to I can be alone. Sometimes I need this; without it I feel bad. It's clear that in my horoscope there are sufficient factors (especially Mercury) to encourage exposure but for me it shouldn't be excessive. That supports my profession of being there for others. It was the same with my mother. She ran a little hairdressers and was well known because her door was open for everybody. People came to have their hair cut because, deep down, they had problems. She was a kind of mother confessor with rational arguments based on esoteric knowledge.

It would seem that this retreat was not always sufficient:

> With a sensitive nature, as reflected in the chart, how do I deal with being very much in the public eye? That's the most difficult part. I don't believe I always manage terribly well. A lot is demanded of me considering my sensitivity. For 30 years, while I gave classes, I was always there for others. I was there at every moment… and that was too much. I couldn't resist. In the depths of my unconscious shattered residues were accumulating. In 1991, I had a heart attack and now I have this tumour.

In addition to the constant work, were these hidden tensions of aggression and sensitivity another contributory factor in Bruno's heart attack and subsequent illness? We will never know.

---

122 Bachmann, Op.Cit. Bruno Huber interview.

Bruno, smoker

What we do know is that Bruno was an inveterate and unapologetic smoker, which is a known causative factor in heart problems and cancers.

Photo Harald Zittlau

Rita Keller lived for a while in the API Centre's top floor flat with her daughter Andrea. Sometimes Andrea would come back home late at night. If the door to Bruno's office was open she would see him always "sat in a blue haze, thinking and writing".[123]

Typical Bruno!

123 Landolt, Btuno, "Zum 20. Todestag von Bruno Huber", Astrolog 231, Oct 2019, page 13. Story told by Andrea at Bruno's funeral.

8. Maturity and Transformation

1992-2009

Change of Pace

Bruno's heart attack in 1991 forced a complete change of pace. The whirlwind of activity had to slow down, and Michael Huber stepped up to take some of the load off Bruno. Louise continues the story[125].

> In 1991 everything suddenly changed, as Bruno had a heart attack and we had to take things more easily. All the travelling had to stop.
>
> Our son Michael took over the majority of Bruno's teaching work and threw himself into keeping API going.
>
> During the 1990s, we also added to the API teaching staff, and handed over some of our courses to them.

Production of regular issues of *Astrolog* continued through the efforts of sub-editor Rita Keller. In 1997 *Astrolog* reached its 100th issue, celebrated by a special cover containing images of the front covers of earlier editions, many incorporating Bruno's photographs or artwork.

When the cover of that edition is spread out, the images of Roberto Assagioli and Bruno Huber appear side by side.

125 Louise Huber, *DAP*, page 19.

The Hubers' books were continuing to spread and sell well, such that by early 1998 there were editions of various books available in German, English, Spanish, Norwegian, French, Portuguese, Italian, Polish, Russian and Croatian. It was reported that worldwide there had been by that time altogether 305,000 books available on the market[126].

Bruno takes it easy

Bruno did not stop completely, in that he continued to give some talks and make overseas visits to England and Spain. Louise took the main load, but Bruno continued to give inspirational talks, such as those at their last joint seminar in England, 1998, on *Astrology and the Seven Rays*. During this seminar his inspiration was undiminished, but it was noticeable that he retreated to their room to rest when not directly involved in the teaching.

In 1998 came celebrations in Zürich for the 30th anniversary (Jubilee) of the formation of API.

API 30th anniversary Photo: Harald Zittlau

Towards the end of the decade Bruno was diagnosed with a cancer, which was to prove fatal. He explained how he was taking the possibility of his approaching death[127].

> There are two angles. On the one hand, now I can and must concentrate with increasing clarity on what I hold in my heart. On

126 Louise Huber, 'Der Werdegang des API', *Astrolog* 103 Apr 1998, page 7.
127 Bachmann, Op. Cit. Bruno Huber interview.

the other hand, I must retire from the front line. I no longer give classes. I am here for now.

At this time I am facing death. The doctor who diagnosed the tumour said that nowadays cancer doesn't necessarily imply death. Something can be done. And that is what I'm doing, I'm doing everything possible, I'm fighting death. I still want to do things but I'll accept it when it comes. My strength could come to an end at any moment.

Death is not a barrier for me.

I've completed my creative work. It has been born.

Bruno dies

Bruno Huber died on 3rd November 1999. It was with heavy heart that the leaders of the English and Spanish Huber Schools joined German-speaking members of the API family, friends and kinfolk at Bruno's funeral in Adliswil.

Photo: Harald Zittlau

Some of the tributes to this inspirational human being from many members of the astrological-psychological Huber family are on page 142 onwards.

Completion of the Huber Books

In 1992 there were still aspects of the Huber teachings that had not been made available in book form. Louise and Michael ensured that the complete set of volumes became available.

Transformation

In 1996 the original *Life Clock III* was significantly revised and republished as *Transformation*[128]. It aims to "use the individual horoscope as a way to wholeness, to synthesis and spiritual development" and highlights a number of techniques that can help in this process.

Aspect Patterns

Publication of a book on aspect patterns was delayed until it was possible to print in colour, which the Hubers saw as essential to understanding what it was about. The Aspect Pattern book[129] was finally published in German with full colour illustrations in 1999. The aspect pattern reveals deep motivations of the personality. Over 45 different aspect patterns are identified, each with its own characteristic meaning.

The Hubers saw this book as "the key to holistic horoscope interpretation and to the understanding of people's true essence.[130]" The foreword suggests that this is a major advance for astrology[131]:

> This book arose from the need for holistic guidelines for astrological-psychological horoscope interpretation. Up to now, nearly all interpretation books have simply described individual aspects, which often contradict each other. This book should enable you to learn to interpret the horoscope as a whole.
>
> This book is founded on the revolutionary discovery that aspect patterns in themselves have an important motivational significance. They are of overriding importance and serve as synthesizing generic terms for the interpretation of the individual planets within them.

---

128 Bruno & Louise Huber, *Transformation: Astrology as a Spiritual Path*, HopeWell 2008. First published in German as *Tranformationen*, 1996.

129 Bruno & Louise Huber, *Aspect Pattern Astrology*, HopeWell, 2019 (colour). First published German 1999 (colour), and by HopeWell in English 2005 (black-white).

130 Huber, Op.Cit. *Aspect Pattern*, pages *vii-viii.*

131 *ibid.*

Thus was realised Bruno's original intuition of the gestalt that lay within the birth chart.

The Planets

The planets are of course a key part of astrological interpretation. The Hubers have a rich interpretation of their meaning, in both psychological and spiritual terms. This next book explains the psychological meaning of the planets related to their positioning in the horoscope[132]. This includes the vital concepts of tool, ego and transpersonal planets, and of the level of consciousness at which a planet is operating in the person's life. Louise describes its significance thus[133]:

> This volume, dealing with the functionality of the ten planets, is particularly important for the interpretation of the horoscope. The planets represent fundamental archetypal qualities that are present in everyone and enable us to live a conscious life. They are the cornerstone in the building of the horoscope, and influence each of its five levels. The position of the ten planets in a zodiac sign, in a house and with certain aspects, allows accurate psychological observations to be made about people, and also informs us on how to live a successful life.

This completed the series of 8 volumes on astrological psychology begun with *The Astrological Houses* in 1975 – a timespan of nearly 30 years.

Astro Glossarium

At the time of his death, Bruno was in the process of compiling his *Astro Glossarium*, a compendium of astrological terms, references and meanings. Extracts were released in the magazine *Astrolog*, and eventually *Volume I (A-G)* was published in German. This was intended to contain the sum of Bruno's knowledge and know-how, and the results of all his research into everything astrological. New material continued to accumulate in issues of *Astrolog*, but unfortunately, due to Bruno's untimely death, this masterwork was never completed[134].

---

132 Bruno & Louise Huber, *The Planets and their Psychological Meaning: Capabilities and Tools of the Personality*, HopeWell, 2006. First published German 2002.

133 Huber, ibid, page 1.

134 Bruno Huber, *Astro Glossarium I*, API Verlag 1995, reported by Wolfhard König in the *Glossarium* entry for 'Bruno Huber', *Conjunction Digest III*, page 57, 58. This volume has not been translated into English to date.

Bruno's attitude to this work was revealed in his last interview[135]:

> I know it's something important but inwardly I'm distanced from it. I've assembled the knowledge I've accumulated throughout my life. I've united and structured all that knowledge like a jigsaw puzzle. I've brought together a lot of astrology. It won't be easy to imitate me. And I've written this because there isn't a meaningful dictionary of astrology. I want everything I know to be available to the astrological community, but for me this is not a creative piece of work.

The Seven Rays

The Hubers' explorations into spirituality went further than the books so far published. The esoteric subject of Astrology and the Seven Rays was the subject of their last seminar together in England, in 1998. A transcript of this inspirational and hugely popular seminar was produced by the English School, and later translated into German and published with additional material, which also went into the English version[136]. Louise's foreword expresses its aims.

> The individual lectures give a clear insight into a new and practical approach to the theory of the seven rays, combined with astrology. It is now possible to determine your own individual ray combination and also those of your friends and family. This is a valuable supplement to the theory of Alice Bailey and makes new age esoteric psychology more accessible.
>
> From a spiritual point of view, the study of the seven rays is a search for the original source, the "return to the father's house", which is called the "path of initiation" in esoteric literature. A contribution of esoteric astrology is to use the three spiritual planets to determine the stages, the conversion processes and the expansions of consciousness that must be passed through. The theory of the rays brings an added dimension to this; it taps our spiritual potential and gives us a new sense of identity that enables us to align our lives with the cosmos.

The aim was spiritual development. In the Seven Rays seminar Bruno expressed this as in a way the modern world moving beyond the deep works of Alice Bailey towards a process of self-initiation[137]:

---

135 Bachmann, Op.Cit. Bruno Huber, interview.

136 Bruno & Louise Huber, *Astrology and the Seven Rays*, HopeWell, 2006.

137 Huber, Op. Cit. *Seven Rays*, page 149.

Nowadays self-initiation is in. Each person may undertake to strive forward in trying to grow in consciousness, and then this person will follow the laws of nature that are true not only for the material world but also for the emotional world, for the mental world, for the higher levels of spirit. There are always laws of nature that say "that's possible" and "that's not possible".

There are no people that tell you that you should not do that. You'll find out what doesn't work, and then you'll learn what's the right way to go, and then you go through stages of initiation. You may call it initiation or not, it's not important, but your consciousness will grow. We grow as a result of striving, very often in sudden jumps.

Astrology and the Seven Rays proved to be the last of the Hubers' books.

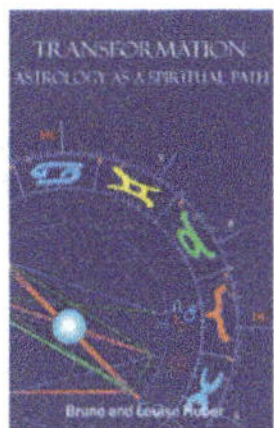

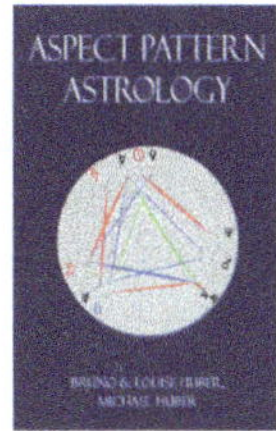

Completing the series – latest English versions: *Transformation*, *Aspect Patterns*, *Planets*; followed by *Seven Rays* and *Astro Glossarium* (German only)

API Endgame

After Bruno's death, Louise continued to drive API forward, supported by Michael Huber, who took on some of Bruno's work, and by Michael's ex-wife Margaretha-Perla[138]. Things almost seemed as before when Michael and Louise came to Wales and gave a seminar in the Brecon Beacons in 2003, but this turned out to be Louise's last visit to the UK.

Michael Huber
2003

Louise takes the API Story up to 2004[139].

Today [2004] we have a teaching staff of about 80 enthusiastic teachers of the Huber method. Because of the organically developed systematic

138 Samantha Breno suggests her mother's significant role, email Oct 2020.

139 Louise Huber, Op. Cit. *DAP*, page 19.

teaching programme, and thanks to Michael's detailed courseware, the course can be taught consistently by all teachers. That is a big advantage in the teaching of the Huber method and makes the future of the API secure.

When Bruno died, Michael and I were thrown back on our own resources. Michael was able to seamlessly take over Bruno's creative, counselling and teaching activities, and continue them successfully. Since 2001, we have been working with two long-term colleagues, Wolfhard König[140] and Ruth Schmidhauser[141], whom we added to the Institute's management team, so that the API is now successfully led by a qualified and dedicated team of four.

API students are led on a process of inner change and learn how to transform petty or egotistical goals. We are partly interested in the ongoing creation of a new ethic in astrology, but also with making the psychological and humanitarian aspects of astrology known to a wider public. As such, the demands we make of our students are high. After 36 years of teaching activity, nearly 10,000 students have passed through the API and the Huber schools in the UK and Spain, and new ones are always coming. We have therefore had to keep hiring new people, and not stand still, but rather to keep on growing with our new students. This keeps us alive and hopefully young!

Now in 2004, after 36 years we have reached the DC in the API horoscope, and the Age Point is transiting the unaspected Saturn. That is a clear message that we should

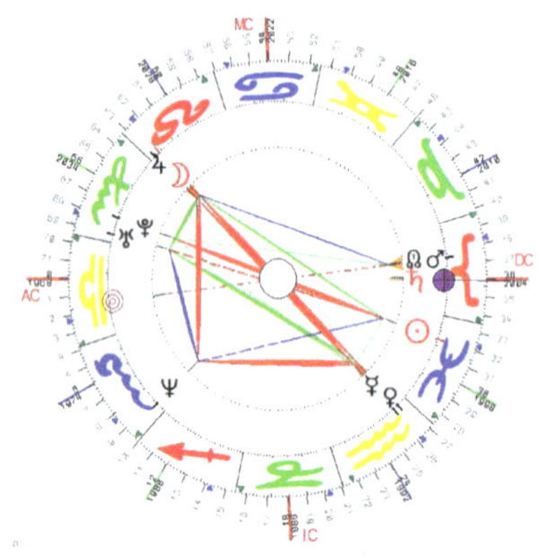

API Switzerland
AP at DC, February 2004

140 Wolfhard König: born 1948, Oberau. Psychologist specialising in depth psychology, psychotherapy and astrology. Taught at Munich University. Huber teacher and long term collaborator since 1974. (From König, Op. Cit. Bruno Huber, *Conjunction*, page 18.)

141 Ruth Schmidhauser / Stüssi: Long term practice of polarity therapy, psychosynthesis, family counselling and astrological psychology teacher with API. (From *Astrolog* 182, Aug 2011, page 32.)

not shirk from the constant stimulation of this human contact, but instead remain open and ready to give of our best. We know from our rules of interpretation that unaspected planets always have a special significance. As Saturn is associated with the promoting of steady, secure relationships, with regard to the You relationship, it indicates that we should not give up on our endeavours, but persist in the face of resistance. After 36 years of uninterrupted activity, we have created a strong, durable structure that provides security. We are grateful for the trust of many long-standing friends who have given and still give us the confidence and strength to continue with our work.

Many people benefit from the results of the research with which Roberto Assagioli aided us, and which Bruno and Michael further developed to create a viable concept of the human being. Today the continued existence of a dedicated API teaching staff is ensured for the future, in particular due to Michael's motivation. He deserves my special thanks, because together we have created a new astrology that is relevant for the New Age. We have therefore come full circle "like a spiral", what was started can now flow back and out into the world to bring the hearts and minds of the people together. Astrological psychology has already been an "accessible path to the self" for many people. I hope and wish that it will help many more people, as it has helped me, to come to terms with themselves and to become a whole person.

Louise reflects

In 2003 Louise reflected on this period[142]:

The loss of Bruno

Michael, our son, has taken charge of much of what Bruno did for API. For me, that is a great gift. Personally I am in spiritual contact with Bruno. But I don't want to speak too much about that. From the personal perspective, the vacuum is not too great… it is simply that Bruno is not here physically. Having always been with people since childhood, for the first time in my life I am alone. But this does not make me suffer, on the contrary, I enjoy being alone.

142 Bachmann, Op. Cit. Louise interview.

The esoteric

Twenty or thirty years ago, when I spoke about karma and reincarnation in my lectures, Bruno whispered in my ear: "Don't talk about that!" In those days, such themes were not talked about widely, whereas today esotericism is in the street. In antiquity, there were mystery schools. Later, Helena Blavatsky published *The Secret Doctrine* (1888), and last century Alice Bailey appeared on the scene. Now such questions are in the public domain. This forms part of the divine plan. The human being has matured much. Thank God!

Evolution of astrology

Astrology is an expansive concept that is continually evolving. Although we have developed the Huber Method with its rules, we are always open to possible innovations. For example, we are now integrating the theme of transformation – a developmental process on four levels. All the components of the horoscope can be interpreted at four levels (physical, emotional, mental, transformation). For example we interpret the planets, not only from a material perspective but also at psychic, mental, and transformational levels. This theme is detailed in our last book, *The Planets*, because today's human being can understand the four dimensions so much better than in the past. The majority of people increasingly reject polarized thinking in terms of black and white and are more interested in questions of evolution and the meaning of the Whole.

Underlying concepts

The concepts of Alice Bailey have always been fundamental, as has the psychosynthesis of Roberto Assagioli. The Tibetan spoke of three horoscopes and we work with three horoscopes. For me, this demonstrates that what we are doing is right. Aspect patterns are something else. I have a quadrangular structure and Bruno a more triangular one. At first I wanted to change Bruno into a quadrangular type and behave as though I had a triangular structure. When we understood that each one of us must live our own aspect picture, we began to be more creative. This experience enabled us to transmit to our students from the start that they should not seek to manipulate or change the aspect structure.

Self healing

Our work and our conceptual astrological model are oriented towards self-healing (self-awareness and self-therapy). We have seen the results in our students. After three years of training they are new people (without us having influenced their developmental process). It happens universally through a conceptual astrological model.

Astrological psychology and other approaches

Our astrology is itself a psychology. Bruno attributed great importance to the name. We do not follow the methodical principles of Jung, Adler, or others. Bruno developed a psychological method, so we call it astrological psychology. In contrast, the representatives of psychological astrology aim to incorporate Jungian concepts or methods, or transactional analysis into their life scripts.

Seen from the evolutionary perspective, every approach has its place. Astrology is multi-faceted. You have your place, I have mine, Liz Greene has hers, as has Elizabeth Teissier. There comes a point where you should not judge or attack those who do not think the same way as you.

Nevertheless, the opposition phase (which is part of every developmental process) is also important and, when we are in it, the first thing we do is fire off at others. This is part of a three-dimensional process: at the first level, we encounter blindness, at the second level polarization, and at the third level we achieve understanding.

The future of API

The preservation of API is important to me, to leave it so that it can autonomously grow. That is why I continue being so active. But I still do not have a clear vision as to whether API will last as an institution or only survive in spirit.

If the latter, this would mean that a large number of people used the organic concept of astrological psychology in harmony with evolutionary thinking. Many people would benefit from it, living more globally, knowing themselves better, and treating their peers with greater understanding. This would facilitate expansion of consciousness without necessarily depending on API as an institution. API's concept can be assimilated by many more people because it is systematized, so anyone can use it.

I don't know what will happen to the API institute, how long it will continue to exist. That will depend on Michael and my grandchildren. It's in the hands of divine will. I have completed my task and, when I look back, I see a life in which I have accomplished my mission.

Personal desires

In reality, I have had three incarnations in this life and soon I will be 80... What more do I want? Perhaps I could still interiorize all that I have done in my life...

End of an Era

API struggles

2004 proved a difficult year for API financially, and a reduced level of activity became necessary[143]. Slowly the organisation foundered, as the driving force of Louise began to wane. She was now over 80 years old.

The API 7th house Low Point in 2008 signalled its 40th anniversary, and celebrations were held in Switzerland, but as the huge gap at the top of the API Switzerland chart shows, there were no tools to continue. A different way had to be found.

API Switzerland and IFAP

Over the years 2005-8 there developed conflicts within the leadership team[144]. Essentially, Michael Huber wanted to run API himself, incorporating some of his own new ideas into its teaching, disconnected from API International. The other leaders wanted to continue with a more collegiate style and the established courses, continuing to be linked with API International. Matters came to a head in 2008/9.

In the end, Louise gave the API organisation to Michael, but left the other teachers free to go their own way with API International, which, now under Wolfhard König, continued to maintain the professional course structure outwith API, including the provision of common summer schools (Achberg). API International was reformed as a professional association with a new constitution, and in August 2009 was renamed Internationaler Fachverband für Astrologische Pychologie (IFAP)[145].

The API company formally closed down in 2009.

---

143 Summarised in 'Die Erfolgsgeschichte des API', Louise Huber/Bruno Landolt, *Astrolog* 210 Apr/May 2016.

144 Events leading up to the closure of API described by Harald Zittlau in personal communication, and by Wolfhard König written submission Oct 2020..

145 Fachverband = Professional Association.

A further development in 2011 saw the evolution into a number of separate schools and institutes in the German-speaking area offering individual courses and Diplomas, within the context of API International. The Swiss/German Huber schools also became part of Netzwerk Astrologische Psychologie[146], a loosely connected communication network.

Distance Learning School

With the closure of API, the old API correspondence course was left homeless. Elke Gut and Harald Zittlau got together to create a completely revised new internet-based distance learning school, within the IFAP framework. This provides for both online study through a web portal and correspondence working[147].

Astrolog continues

Astrolog had continued to be published by API since Bruno's death, edited by Rita Keller. But after Issue 166 Louise decided that it could no longer be afforded and planned to close it down[148]. Rita Keller was also ready to retire. Bruno Landolt tells what happened[149]:

> Wolfhard König realized that without the magazine the association would lose its meaning. Bruno Landolt and Harald Zittlau were commissioned to find a solution to keep *Astrolog* alive. A meeting was organized in Frankfurt with a professional editor. A new operation had to be set up from scratch, with the next release date 6 weeks away. We needed to fill 40 pages of content, find authors, establish a modern layout using new software, and find an affordable printing service. This new team delivered Issue 168 on time, and the new look was widely accepted. We were on track. Bruno Landolt then took over as editor, learning how to build everything himself.

Astrolog thus set off with new energies, which continue to this day[150]. The rights to publish *Astrolog* had been transferred to IFAP in 2009[151].

---

146 Meyer, Eslbeth, 'Netzwerk Astrologische Psychologie', *Astrolog* 207, Nov 2015.

147 Elke Gut, submission to editors, Oct 2020.

148 Landolt, Bruno, 'Rückblick auf eine Erfolgsgeschichte', *Astrolog* 200, Aug 2014.

149 Landolt, Bruno, submission to editors, Oct 2020.

150 Wolfhard Konig, 'Der Astrolog', *Astrolog* 166, Nov. 2008, page 16.

151 The publisher API Verlag remained with the Huber family, currently Margaretha-Perla Huber (now Sicher).

Michael & Louise

Despite the closure of API, it would seem that Louise's wish was fulfilled, in that the Huber Method and system of teaching live on and continue to flourish through the above arrangements.

Michael Huber continued with some teaching activities, including a number of seminars in Spain on his new idea of 'planetology'[152], but in 2011 the API House in Adliswil was sold and Michael moved with his partner to Salzbergen in northern Germany. After this time Michael was no longer visibly active in astrological psychology.

Louise moved to a retirement home in Switzerland, no longer active. In 2013 the family moved Louise to another retirement home in Salzbergen[153] to live out the rest of her days.

Death of Louise

Louise Huber died on 13th January 2016 at 12:45 in Salzbergen, just after her AP passed by Pluto for the second time, 72 years after the end-of-war experience set her on her spiritual path. Transformation indeed!

Tributes from some of the people who have been inspired along the way by Bruno & Louise are on page 142 onwards.

152 Re Michael Huber's 'planetology', see also .page 135.

153 Information on Louise's retirement from Harald Zittlau, September 2020.

9. The English Huber School

Inspiration

A young American astrologer, Pamela Tyler, became inspired by the Hubers and their approach and was instrumental in getting English astrologer Richard Llewellyn interested.

Pam Tyler and the Hubers

Pam tells how it all started[155].

> My first meeting with Bruno and Louise Huber was at the 1978 AFA Convention in Atlanta[156]. Bruno's brief lecture on the Huber Method was a fortuitous moment in my own astrological development. I had come from London to sit for the AFA Teacher Certification examination and was scheduled to do the Faculty of Astrological Studies Diploma exam the next year. I was a passionate 'autodidact' familiar with every imaginable astrological technique, but the Huber vision changed that obsession. So many things caught my interest: the aspect structure's explicit significance for motivation, the

Bruno, Louise, Pam Tyler, England

155 Pam Tyler, email to editors, May 2020.

156 This was Bruno & Louise's first conference in USA.

Dynamic Energy Curve's revelatory explanation of why traditional house placements do not always yield a promised result (e.g. Sun in the 10th house equals a high-profile career), and Age Progression's value for pinpointing focus for a person's chronological age. Age Progression was especially helpful when clients thirty years my senior sought counsel, even more so if they had uncertain birth times. The Huber contribution was both awe inspiring and humbling.

It was plain that the more I knew the less I really understood about that great mystery called human nature. But I sensed that Bruno and Louise were onto something different...

Like many seasoned astrologers who discovered the Huber work, I was leery about accepting Saturn as Mother and the wholesale rejection of Progressions and Transits. But I did so for a season. The Huber Method required sticking to the 'program'. You could not add or subtract what suited you. It was a bit like piano lessons which demanded daily practice of the Hanon scales – onerous but essential if one ever wanted to be 'free from the keyboard.' Converting client files by hand to Huber style took some time.

But it was through that exercise plus a renewed attention to my own horoscope that the marvel of the method unfolded. Not only did new insights abound, but my confidence in astrology's psychological value grew ten-fold.

The Hubers at Sarnen

I went twice to Sarnen, the first time as a newbie Huber student and the second time as Louise's *Aide de Camp*. Both workshops focused on the Huber basics. Bruno and Louise did the lectures but it was my job to assist the students in applying Huber principles to their natal charts. My limited Huber expertise made this a bonus learning opportunity for me as students shared sudden "Ah hah" epiphanies in the process. Because Sarnen participants varied in technical skill, psychological sensitivity, professional experience as well as cultural background, internalizing Huber practice involved more than straightforward lectures. Some of the most transformative work came in the more informal meditative or creative sessions.

The Hubers In England

The English astrological world in the early 80s was a vibrant bustling community. The Astrological Association and The Astrological Lodge held regular London meetings and similar gatherings throughout the UK. Formal astrological education abounded and with it an increasing effort to professionalize the practice of astrology. Credentials as an astrologer were important. Traditional astrology flourished along with singular efforts to 'prove' astrology scientifically as did an emerging academic interest in its history. While these educational programs filled the need for learning the basics, no one school excelled in teaching how to balance multiple horoscope factors. Liz Greene's Jungian psychological astrology certainly influenced astrologers but obtaining certification required substantial personal Jungian therapy.

The Hubers' astrological psychology emphasized in depth knowledge of one's own horoscope. But it did not require outside psychotherapy for diploma certification. What it did though was to provide a systematic means for seeing the horoscope holistically and the skills to synthesize complex layers of meaning. Particularly appealing from my viewpoint was the empty circle at the center of the chart.

There the Huber' philosophical and psychological regard for human autonomy and free will takes precedence. Neither an astrologer's curiosity nor a planetary opposition can penetrate this domain uninvited. This profound respect for human beings found fertile ground in Devon.

One short weekend course attracted Richard and Alice Llewellyn's fervent support. Richard Llewellyn caught the vision and fortunately ran with it as my days in England were numbered.

Establishing the School

1983-1991

Richard Llewellyn follows through

Richard Llewellyn takes up the story of how the English Huber School came into being[157].

> In Spring 1981 Richard Llewellyn had resigned from his work in industry having decided to practise as an astrologer, tutor for the Mayo School, and also work on material which he was recording as a series of audio tapes for teaching astrology. In the autumn of that year he met with Pamela Tyler, an American astrologer working in London. Pam was in Devon, and staying with Richard and his wife Alice, to run a weekend workshop in a "new" approach to chart interpretation – the Huber Method – which Pam had encountered at a seminar in Switzerland, run by Bruno & Louise Huber, earlier in the year.
>
> The workshop generated much enthusiasm and Pam encouraged Richard to go to Switzerland the following year to attend another 5 day introductory seminar which the Hubers were to run in Sarnen following the first World Astrology Congress in Zürich at Easter. Feeling that the "traditional" approach he was teaching was sterile, he made the decision to go and, in Richard's words, it turned out to be the turning point in his life. For him the psychological approach suddenly gave purpose and meaning to astrology.

Richard
Sarnen 1982

> **Bringing the material to a wide audience**
>
> Although this seminar was in English the Hubers normally taught only in German at classes held in their home in Adliswil and Pam and Richard felt that their psychological approach deserved a wider audience.

157 Richard Llewellyn, 'How the English Huber School Came Into Being,' *Conjunction* 58, page 24.

They talked this over and at a meeting in a Knightsbridge pub in London on 8th June 1983 at 12:30pm made the decision to found the English Huber School and write some simple material which students could build on themselves. Amongst the decisions agreed was that, during the course, students would work on their own chart as well as that of their tutor and a friend who was well known to them. With hindsight this was probably an important ingredient which greatly contributed to the successes which the School's Diploma Course has achieved.

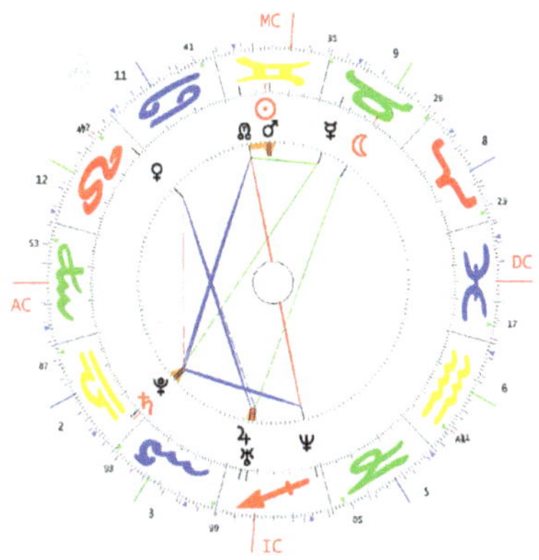

Founding of English Huber School

Pam and Richard discussed the content of the Lessons which each agreed to write. This would entail acquiring a deep understanding of the Hubers' approach, since Bruno and Louise taught verbally and there was at that time no material available to translate. The English School Manuals would have to be created from nothing, and this mainly entailed editing notes made at various opportunities to meet with the Hubers at their home in Switzerland and at seminars which were subsequently arranged for them in England.

Core Group

The initial stages of this project did not work out quite as planned since Pam was accepted as a student at Law School in USA and became immersed in her studies there, so Richard was faced with the task of creating the teaching manuals himself. At that time, he and Alice were holding periodic meetings in their home in Totnes, Devon, attended by a small group of astrologers who had become interested in the Huber approach. Richard invited these early devotees to become involved with the new School and it was from them that the first School Council was formed. They became an integral part of the early years of the School acting as a sounding board for Richard's writing and some, including Val Burnham, Suzanne Deuter, Marcus Mason, Jonathan Powell, Joan Swallow and Brian Vickery, made valuable contributions to the content of the teaching manuals.

Bruno's Amphora, Exeter 1984

The task of creating the first set of teaching manuals, a *Diploma Course in Astrology*, was larger than originally envisaged and wasn't completed until the end of 1984. The first student was enrolled in February 1985. Bruno and Louise came to England at Easter that year and ran a 5 day seminar at Dartington in Devon, as a result of which the School enrolled more students. In the years that followed School Council members, who also became the first tutors, ran workshops introducing this new approach to astrology and chart interpretation in various locations in the UK and overseas. Almost invariably there was an enthusiastic response, whether from beginners or experienced astrologers, and so the School grew.

School Council, 1990, Totnes

Richard eventually decided that a Foundation course was necessary for potential students who had no previous astrological knowledge, so he wrote the Foundation courses which are still [1988] being used. Over the years there have been many evolving changes in the Courses and an increasing emphasis on the need for astrologers to

> acquire counselling skills to work with clients and this is the path the School continues to follow today. Didactic seminars have progressed to experiential workshops and these have become an integral part of the School's teaching. They have also provided an opportunity for students to meet and get to know one another in depth, contributing to the development of the strong "family" feeling amongst students and tutors.
>
> The School became a member of the Advisory Panel on Astrological Education in 1987, and is [1988] actively engaged in providing, promoting and supporting high quality astrological education.

The new English Huber School, also known as API(UK), initially flourished, attracting large numbers of students who were inspired by direct contact with the Hubers when they gave regular seminars in England. The formula was different from API, in that the course was by correspondence. There were 24 lessons with tutor-marked assignments submitted by mail, 4 moderated assessed assignments, 4 mandatory workshops held at annual Face-to-Face events, supplemented by local workshops provided by individual tutors, and a final Diploma presentation. The whole process typically took 3 years.

First Face-to-Face, Totnes 1989

Richard also established a single page news sheet, that eventually morphed into the astrological psychology magazine *Conjunction* that has been published 2-3 times per year since then.

The UK Astrological World

The Hubers, and later on members of the English Huber School, spoke regularly at conferences of the UK Astrological Association, but were always greeted with some scepticism. Most astrologers were conservatively based in medieval approaches, or followed different psychological approaches such as Liz Greene's, more inspired by Jung.

The charts were different, aspect patterns had strange meanings, age progression was different, orbs were special, only certain aspects were used, no planetoids, it was only psychological... and the biggest bone of contention – association of Saturn with the mothering principle.

There were more balanced commentators, such as this assessment of the newly created English Huber School and its courses by well respected astrologer and former AA president Charles Harvey[158].

> The advent of a major new astrology correspondence course into the English-speaking market is something of an event. This is a fully fledged, professionally produced course backed by a sophisticated School Council and an integrated program of seminars, which lead on to the award of the Swiss API's Diploma. The production team and tutorial staff is a group of highly professional individuals, with a strong component of counselling expertise.

Charles Harvey

> Based on over 25 years of teaching and client-centred research and experience by Bruno and Louise Huber, it presents a methodical approach to the Hubers' brand of psychological astrology. This course is clearly here to stay and will add its own stamp to the evolution and development of astrology in the English-speaking world, as it has already to the German-speaking astrological community where over 8,000 students have already studied under this system.

Harvey went on to assess details of the Huber Course and its place in the spectrum of astrological education as a whole.

> Like many recent developments, the course concentrates on the application of astrological principles to psychological counselling, emphasising astrology's power as a tool for developing self-awareness

158 Charles Harvey, 'The English Huber School', *Astrological Journal*, 1985 (edited).

> and personal growth. Those with a broad general background in astrology, who have perhaps attended a Huber seminar and are already attracted to the Hubers' approach need not hesitate. This is the course for them. It is clearly written, well put together and attractively presented so that the Hubers' ideas come over more clearly and coherently than in their own books. The course will give the student a clear grasp of the Hubers' approach to any chart. It also gives them an opportunity to work with their tutor applying the principles they are learning to their own chart and to the charts of other individuals known to them.
>
> The uncommitted would-be student will want to see the benefits and drawbacks of embarking upon this course rather than another. First, it has to be said that this tends to be a "closed system"... which mitigates against the universality of outlook which astrology implies.
>
> For example, in developing its own valuable correlation between the aspect patterns, planets and colour the course only considers aspects which are a multiple of 30°. Students ought to know that other schools place great emphasis on other aspects. To be fair, the introductory course does emphasise that "there are no hard and fast rules in chart interpretation – only guidelines" and does recommend a wide range of further reading.
>
> Other examples of relatively unqualified particularity are in the area of orbs for aspects, Koch houses, Age Progression, the attribution of Saturn to Mother, the 'dynamic energy curve' and 'stress planets'...
>
> Criticisms aside, these are well-constructed and imaginatively presented courses. If you are considering embarking upon professional training in psychologically oriented astrology this Course deserves serious consideration as part of your studies. However, the nature of astrology demands that each student should in a sense adopt the Medieval model and obtain the widest range of viewpoints. The student reared exclusively on the Huber, or any other single school, would not be doing justice to themselves or astrology.

Those who come to astrology through the Huber Method may well not agree with Harvey's analysis – there is enough in this system to take many years to master and harvest its fruits. However, to an astrologer this assessment is reasonably balanced, and puts the Hubers in the context of other astrological approaches.

Steady State

1991-2003

In 1991, Richard passed the school on to new Principal, Joyce Hopewell. Richard remained closely involved as *Principal Emeritus*, and the good work continued. The AP for the English School was appropriately approaching the Saturn-Pluto conjunction, symbolising transformation to new structures.

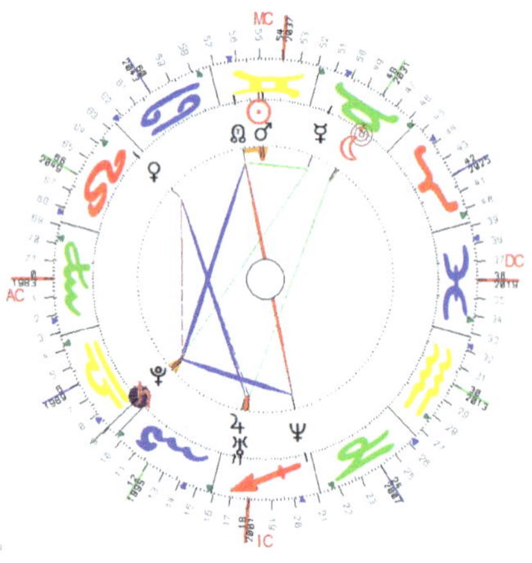

API(UK) chart showing AP cj Pluto

A student in South Africa, Colin Wilton, soon established the School's first website, which has evolved through various incarnations into the today's website.

Regular visits by the Hubers provided inspiration for each new tranche of students, in addition to enthusiastic facilitation by Richard, Joyce and other tutors. The venue for these events and Face-to-Face became the Beacon Centre near Exeter.

1995 API(UK) tutors with Louise & Bruno at Beacon Centre

The highlight perhaps came in 1998 with the hugely popular workshop on *Astrology and the Seven Rays,* which was, sadly, to be Bruno's last visit to England. Fortunately there was the opportunity to celebrate and make a presentation in thanks to Bruno & Louise.

1998 Celebration at 7 Rays Workshop
Elly Gibbs, Joyce, Louise, Bruno, Richard

With Bruno's death in 1999, the brightest attractor of new students in the UK had disappeared. Face-to-Face moved to Buckland Hall in the Brecon Beacons, Wales in 2000, and in 2001 Wolfhard König effectively stood in for the Hubers, coming to give a seminar at Buckland Hall, judge Diploma presentations and help celebrate the 18th birthday of the English school.

2001 Wolfhard König
with Jeremy Cooper

In 2003 Louise came to Buckland Hall with Michael Huber, in what proved to be their last visit to the UK, to give a seminar on *Transformation*, and the last API Switzerland Diploma presentations.

2003 Buckland Hall, Wales
The last API Diploma presentations in UK

Astrological Psychology Association

2003 – 2020

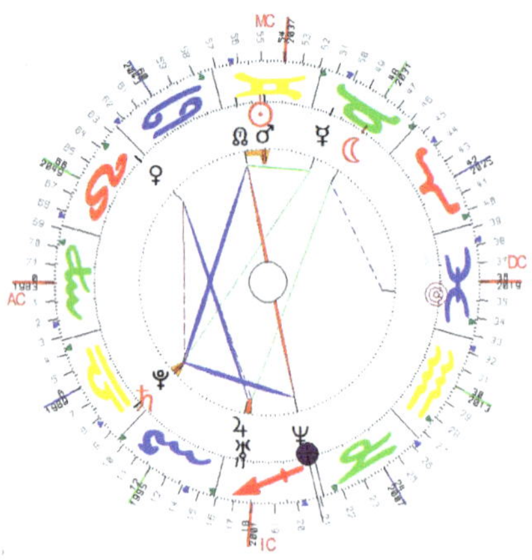

API(UK) chart showing AP cj Neptune

With reducing inspirational input from Switzerland, numbers of enrolments on the courses were slowly declining over this period, with a corresponding reduction in the supply of willing helpers.

When Joyce needed to stop running her own business, an Astrological Psychology Association (APA) was formed in 2003 to carry forward the teaching. It is noticable that the API(UK) AP is here approaching Neptune, after which there is a large gap on the You-side of the chart.

From here on courses were administered first by David Kerr and then by Ghislaine Adams, with Joyce and Richard remaining as guiding lights.

When it became clear that, with Louise now over 80, it was no longer appropriate to rely on the Hubers awarding the Swiss Diploma, the Association necessarily began to issue its own *Diploma in Astrological Psychology*.

There was still the interest and a fair supply of willing students, but not at a level that would sustain the Face-to-Face workshops, which were eventually dropped in 2008. The Association also ran several conferences, the last of which was in 2008 in Manchester.

Incorporation

Following a further reorganisation as a Scottish Limited Company in 2008 (with the API UK AP approaching square to Pluto/Saturn) APA continued the School at a lowish level of activity until 2019.

When it became clear that the level of interest was insufficient to sustain its operation awarding the professional Diploma, it was decided to publish the courses[159] and simply offer freelance teaching/tutoring through the current tutors. The last Diploma awards were completed at the end of 2019. Teaching in astrological psychology remains available in a similar way, but without the formal professional qualification that Richard and Joyce had originally strived so hard to establish.

The *zeitgeist* had moved on in the UK.

The Association remains a membership association for all interested in astrological psychology, with its main manifestation in the website and associated social media, available to supplement any seeker's astrological/psychological/spiritual studies. The Association also has a bookshop and produces the magazine *Conjunction.*

The Books in English

Barry Hopewell outlines the origins of the publisher HopeWell[160].

> When Louise and Michael gave a seminar at Buckland Hall in Wales in 2003 it had become apparent that the Hubers' English publisher Samuel Weisèr was running down publication of their books in English, another indication of the *zeitgeist* of the times. This meant that students of the English School might not be able to obtain copies of books that were by now Set Books for the courses. Also, there was no English-language publisher for the Hubers' latest books *Aspect Pattern Astrology* and *The Planets.*
>
> At that time we were investigating publishing an introductory book for astrological psychology, by Joyce Hopewell and Richard Llewellyn. The new technology of 'print on demand' was just becoming a viable and economic proposition, and I was recently retired and had the time to pursue it, so we suggested to Louise that we might publish some of their books in English through our emerging publishing vehicle HopeWell, including collaborating on the translation of *Aspect Pattern Astrology*. It was a pleasure arranging this with Louise.

---

159 The Diploma Course is pubished in the book *Astrological Psychology: The Huber Method*, HopeWell, 2017, and the Foundation Course in the ebook *Foundation Astrology*, available on the APA website.

160 Barry Hopewell, 'Remembering Louise Huber', *Conjunction* 65, May 2016, page 10.

Introduction to Astrological Psychology

First to be published in 2004 was the introductory book *The Cosmic Egg Timer*[161], which aimed to introduce and outline astrological psychology in just under 200 pages. Of necessity, it was published in black-and white to keep the price accessible to newcomers to the subject. A third edition was published in 2018 with the illustrations in full colour; the technology had moved on.

The Huber books

We found a translator, Heather Ross, for *Aspect Pattern Astrology*. The Hubers had waited until colour printing was affordable to publish this book, and were of the opinion that this was necessary to get the message over. Unfortunately, the cost of colour printing with 'print-on-demand' was at that time prohibitive. We persuaded Louise that black-and-white would work if we also made available laminated bookmarks showing the aspect figures in colour. The book was published in 2005 and has since been the best seller of the English books on astrological psychology. A revised colour edition was published in 2019.

Heather Ross also translated *The Planets* (2006). The other Huber books on astrological psychology followed, by adapting and updating the Weiser texts. Thus the full range of Huber titles was again 'in print' in English by 2011.

Members of the English Huber School transcribed the talks Bruno & Louise gave at their last seminar on *Astrology and the Seven Rays* in Devon in 1998. This was eventually turned into a book of the same title (2008). It was also translated into German and published by API Verlag.

Further titles

A range of further titles was subsequently published by HopeWell, supplementing the main Huber works. These included further introductory books by Joyce: *The Living Birth Chart* and *Using Age Progression*, and a small colour reference on the aspect patterns *Aspect Patterns in Colour.*

---

161 Joyce Hopewell & Richard Llewellyn, *The Cosmic Egg Timer: Introducing Astrological Psychology*, HopeWell, 2018, first pub. 2004.

A bequest by Agnes Shellens provided for the publication of two compendiums of articles from *Astrolog*[162], including further articles by Bruno & Louise, translated by Heather Ross.

In 2014 John Grove's book *Dreams and Astrological Psychology* encouraged the use of dream interpretation in the context of astrological psychology, followed up in 2017 by *Life Passages: When Age Point Aspects and Dreams Coincide.*

In 2015 Sue Lewis's book *Astrological Psychology, Western Esotericism, and the Transpersonal* placed the Hubers' astrological psychology into its academic context as part of the stream of Western esotericism and modern psychology.

The English Huber School's Diploma Course was published in 2017 under the title *Astrological Psychology: The Huber Method.*

Details of all these can be found in the bibliography on page 172.

The English Speaking World

The English Huber School has had students from all over the English-speaking world, notably USA, Australia, Canada, South Africa, Hong Kong, India and Israel; also from non-German Europe, including Norway, Sweden, Netherlands, Romania, Italy, Spain, Portugal and Greece. But there has not, to our knowledge, been a critical mass in any one country for an enduring local centre to be established. Sales of the English books have been similarly widespread, but by far the biggest outlets have been the UK and USA. The majority of students of the English Huber School were UK-based, so what of the USA?

USA

Despite many talks by the Hubers at AFA conferences, a number of students from USA completing the courses of the English Huber School and a fair volume of the English books being purchased, astrological psychology has not, so far, caught on in a big way in the USA. Pam Tyler reflects on the Hubers' experiences in the USA, and why so little headway has apparently been made[163].

162 *Astrolog I; Life and Meaning* (2007), *Astrolog II: Family, Relationships and Health* (2009).

163 Pam Tyler, email to editors, May 2020.

The Huber Method never really caught fire on the American astrology scene. It was not for lack of high visibility as the Hubers regularly appeared at the national and international conferences. Their book *Man and His World*[164] had been released by the extremely reputable book publisher Samuel Weiser. They were definitely 'known' in the name recognition sense but more as head of API in Switzerland and the World Congresses than the particulars of Huber astrology.

But America is a really big place. For Huber work to have a significant impact, it would need at least 10-15 API instructors nation-wide.

Some Americans did attend the Sarnen workshops but certainly not enough to implement a Huber revolution in astrology. How many ultimately adopted the Huber perspective or obtained an API Diploma is unclear.

Alas my contribution to Huber work in America was minimal. I just didn't have time. First law school, then law practice followed by seminary and ordination precluded much engagement in astrology. Joyce Hopewell and I led a Huber week-long program in Miami. API Diploma student Kathy Crabbe and I led a similar program in Laguna Beach CA. Several close friends learned Huber method and for those few remaining astrology clients, the Huber perspective illuminated those conversations. I saw Bruno and Louise at astrology conferences in Washington D.C. and New Orleans. We also met up in Sao Paulo for a week-long workshop. They also visited me in Miami but mainly for social reasons. They did wonder what on earth prompted me to become an Episcopal priest.

Of course, I was not the only American privy to Huber astrology. Apart from the challenge of training enough Huber teachers around the U.S.A. to grow the community, the failure to launch in a meaningful way may arise from several other more subtle cultural reasons.

Astrologers, like other professionals, resist change especially if the status quo is yielding relative success. They will gladly test an isolated Huber idea such as the Low Point but refrain from adopting a new framework. Americans intoxicated by a smorgasbord of astrology fare will sample everything but eschew anything which upends their own best convictions or is potentially doctrinaire.

164 Later titled *The Astrological Houses.*

More importantly, American public education in astrological parlance is Mercury or information driven. Standardized tests prevail requiring encyclopedic knowledge for exams. Students learn rote memorization at the expense of the higher critical thinking associated with Jupiter. Insofar as teacher performance evaluations rely heavily on student exam performance, there is little incentive for teaching students how to think much less synthesize material. Students expect instructors to spoon feed the material. Rather than show them how to grapple with the broader, deeper questions and underlying assumptions within a sphere such as English, Math or Astrology, knowledge is pre-packaged fast food. The Hubers' first book (*Man and His World*) eluded many people precisely because it was not a cookbook. Nor was it the astrological equivalent of a popular psychology self-help book. Assimilating Huber principles required time, discipline, and a complete re-tooling of the interpretive process. There was no quick fix.

American ambivalence toward Huber work might also stem from a frankly acquisitive disposition which suggests "The more I have (by way of Asteroids, Hypothetical planets, Arabian Parts, Fixed Stars, Aspects) the more I am" or perhaps the more I know. This "More the Merrier" delusion clutters the mind as much as it does the horoscope appearance. It begins to look more like a messy closet. When denuded of these extras, the horoscope acquires focus. But for those overly wedded to a specific aspect or asteroid, it also brings loss.

South America

Pam also reports that Bruno & Louise also ran workshops in Brazil:

> The last workshop we did together was in Brazil in 1989. Alice and Richard Llewellyn were there too.

1988 Caminas, Brazil Photo Pam Tyler

> The best part was travelling together after the workshop to the magnificent Foz Iguacu.

Time off at Foz Iguazu Photo Pam Tyler

Huber centres have also developed in several Spanish-speaking countries in South America through the courses and events of the Spanish Huber School. See page 125.

10. The Spanish Huber School

Inspiration and Foundation

Angela Wilfart – pioneer

Angela with Louise

Angela Wilfart was perhaps the first in Spain to engage with the Hubers and astrological psychology. She gives her own story on the beginnings of the Spanish school[166].

"There are more things in Heaven and Earth, Horatio, than are dreamt of in your philosophy."

Shakespeare

Quite a huge part of humanity, I believe, becomes aware one day of this truth, more or less early or late in life. This was the case for me, my starting point with astrology, one lovely day in February 1972 in Tenerife, when I met a German tourist, Gabriele, who spent her holidays in the hotel where I was working at that time. We became friendly and it was the day before she left, that our conversation and discussions became more essential and esoteric. A little ashamed and in low voice, she told me, that she was involved with graphology, which was already quite well respected in Germany at that time, and that she was also very much involved in astrology, which was not. She was studying this science in a German School (Ebertin) with psychological, biological, humanitarian aims using traditional, classic interpretations. Our conversation became passionate, and her answers to my numerous questions were logical and convincing.

During the following years I was struggling to find my way in learning something really valid about astrology, without a teacher, and reading unconvincing books, when oh wonder, after several years, Gabriele came once more to Tenerife and offered me the first

166 Input from Angela Wilfart by WhatsApp and email, May 2020.

book of the Hubers published in 1975 *Der Mensch und seine Welt* – I found in it what I was looking for: a better understanding of human psychic behaviour and the relationship between the cosmos and the human being as in fact all life of our planet Earth. I decided to translate this book, first into French and then into Spanish. I wrote to API in Adliswil and went to my first seminar in Achberg in 1977 where I met Bruno, Louise and Michael Huber. The impact of their personality was deep and the seminar impressed me greatly.

I was then 46, just out of the most important Low-Point of the 8th house. I did not yet know anything about Age Progression, but in fact I faced a new challenge in my life and took the new orientation, and opened the way to become a helpful person in using my astro-psychological knowledge for teaching and counselling – hopefully until old age. All this was possible with the loving understanding and sustaining of my husband. But first I had to learn to assist at seminars and attend workshops. In 1981, I was gratified by being awarded the API Diploma. I continued to translate, learn and teach in Spain where we lived at that time, about 50 kms north of Sevilla.

"If you don't feel it, you will not catch it."

Johann Wolfgang von Goethe

Why did Bruno and Louise make such a great impression on me? It was their authenticity, their friendly, accepting, helpful interaction with all they encountered. They were sure of what they were teaching, it was a new model, strongly structured, a new look at interpretation of the horoscope with the psychological symbolism of the planets, the zodiacal signs, the houses and the aspects, and their inter-connection between them and with our centre, our soul – a big network. This was built up during the collaboration with Roberto Assagioli who offered them the living material of his patient's problems so that Bruno and Louise were able to do the link with their own psychological knowledge. After this collaboration they founded the Institute of Astrological Psychology – teaching a new kind of psychology, relating it to our cosmic descendant and our soul, our deepest centre.

Rosa Solé discovers Huber astrology

Rosa Solé Gubianes outlines how she first became interested in Huber astrology, and how the Spanish Huber School came into being[167].

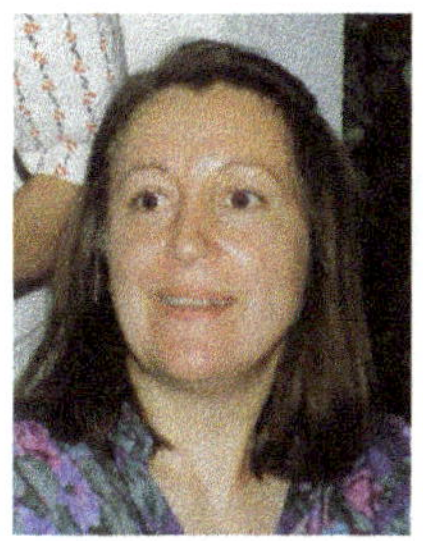

Rosa Solé
Adliswil 1991

My interest in astrology began when I was very young. I learnt from different teachers in Barcelona, but it was not until 1983, when I had the opportunity to live in England, that I started my training in a more professional way at the Faculty of Astrological Studies in London.

In 1985 an advertisement in the Astrological Association magazine caught my attention. It was about a new training in psychological astrology and it led me to get in touch with Richard and Alice Llewellyn of the English Huber School. I remember the long train journey from London to Totnes, a town with a special charm, and my first encounter with them.

In Totnes, I expected to find an old building and a serious and rigid director as in many institutes in Spain at that time. Instead, I was surprised to be received in their home. Their warmth and humbleness made me feel very well received in spite of the fact that my English was awful and my shyness exaggerated my fears and made everything more difficult.

I was impressed with their respect and admiration for the Hubers' work. They told me that it would be better if I introduce myself to them personally before starting the training.

I attended the intensive seminar that Bruno and Louise Huber gave in Sarnen in 1986. Even today I can feel my emotion when listening to Bruno and the certainty I had of learning from his wisdom. Bruno's Uranus in Aries just in the midpoint of my Sun/Moon in Aries too.

Louise and Rosa
1988 Froebel

167 Personal contribution from Rosa Solé Gubianes, May 2020.

In 1987 I enrolled in the distance learning course in the English Huber School. They were magical and intense years of seminars and courses in Totnes, Sarnen, London and Adliswil. Apart from the Hubers' teachings, I feel very grateful for the opportunity I had of learning from the teachers of the English Huber School, for their training in psychosynthesis and their humanistic vision of astrological counselling. In 1989 I obtained the API Diploma in Adliswil and my idea was to become a mentor of the EHS for Spanish students.

Establishment

1990-2001

At the III World Congress held in Luzern in April 1990, after listening Bruno's talk, Angela Wilfart, Richard Llewellyn and myself met [Angela reports that Rosa tried to contact her by megaphone.] Richard launched the proposal "Why not a Spanish Huber School?"

So, in 1990, with the collaboration of Angela Wilfart and Richard Llewellyn, the Spanish Huber School was created: my AP was on Jupiter in Pisces in the seventh house.

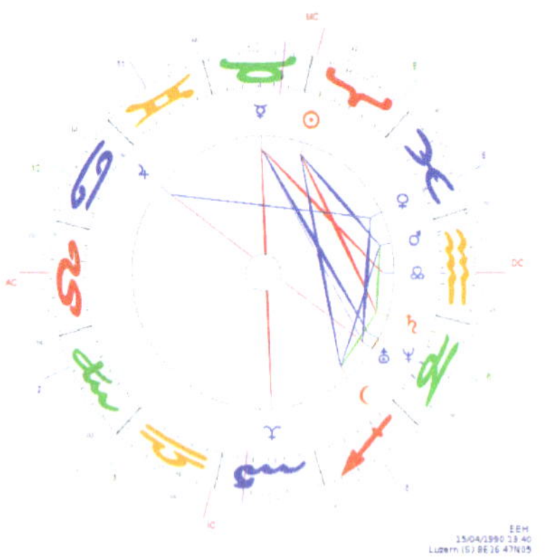

Foundation of Spanish School
15/04/1990, 13:40, Luzern, CH

They were intense years where Bruno and Louise imparted courses in Spain, in 1993 (Caldes de Montbui), 1996 (Xorret del Catí) and 1999 (Liérganes) in which they awarded the diploma to several students who had completed the course.

The distance course was that of the English School, translated into Spanish. Angela Wilfart and Richard Llewellyn supported the course with their experience and by adding different seminars on the Psychology of Colour and Personal Psychosynthesis.

The continued support and help from Richard Llewellyn and later from Joyce Hopewell of the EHS facilitating the growth of the

Xorret del Catí 1996

Spanish Huber School, built in me a personal fantasy of family model, Mother England and Father Switzerland.

Translation – Perfect Synchronicity

Translation was a major necessity for the Spanish school. The materials were available in German and, increasingly, in English. But neither the Hubers nor the English teachers were fluent in Spanish. Fortunately, there came Lola Ferrer, who became a key member of the Spanish school. Here Lola recalls events and impressions[168].

I remember my first contact with the Huber School as one of those once-in-a-lifetime moments of perfect synchronicity.

Luzern spring 1990. I was with a group of friends attending the third World Astrological Congress in Switzerland. We were all enjoying the rich astrological atmosphere, the enthusiasm and the novelty. On the loudspeakers I heard a call in Spanish, a person called Angela Wilfart was requesting Rosa Solé from Barcelona to attend a meeting. So, I thought, there are some more people from home around here...?

Their names were new to me, as were the Hubers, the couple organizing the event, the creators of a new approach to astrology, the Huber Method. I felt a tremendous impulse to find who they were. Little wonder, my Age Point was starting to make a trine to Mercury, while Saturn was sitting on top of it. So I contacted them and met a group of devoted, serious astrologers: Rosa, Angela and Richard Llewellyn from the English Huber School. I learnt later on that

168 Lola Ferrer, 'Remembering Bruno & Louise Huber', by email May 2020.

April 15th was the very day Richard suggested creating a Spanish Huber School, a task that Rosa Solé took on with tremendous drive, love and commitment. The same year in September I was already translating Richard's first psychosynthesis seminar in Barcelona, the first of many we had the privilege to attend. He would become a wonderful friend, mentor, and an ambassador for API.

Bruno & Louise came to Spain to give seminars quite often in the decade of the '90s. And I had the opportunity to discover the beauty and coherence of the Huber system.

I used to translate their seminars into Spanish. I recall three of them at least, an intense and demanding task both satisfying and stimulating. I was by then a student of their Diploma and it was a joy to learn directly from them while translating at the same time, all of which had me deeply immersed in my task. Bruno was brilliant in his explanations. He was very conscious of my needs as a consecutive translator and very attentive that I could manage to pour into correct Spanish his ideas in English. So he had the patience and delicacy to wait for me until I had fully understood and translated each sentence.

He delivered his original concepts with great calm and depth making it easy for me to connect with his ideas. I clearly recall entering into a flowing but intense current of mutual understanding that finally made translating an effortless and pleasant succession of ideas into a coherent body of knowledge. Both of us had our nodes in Aries, and his Uranus was exact conjunct my node! A click of his Venus to my Uranus in the 9th house was also an extra gift of swiftness and electrical understanding which worked to perfection...

With Louise it was quite a different story. She got so passionate in her explanations, her ideas and words had such a power! She was carried away and completely forgot that her Spanish audience could hardly understand her English and that I was unable to follow her fast pace. We tried to stop and remind her from time to time, but she soon forgot about us. When she woke from her train of thought I was often lost and the audience too. To her it was a surprise that we looked so bewildered, which created more than one comic moment after all... Good healthy laughs!

There followed more Seminars, I remember Alicante in 1996, and Liérganes, Cantabria the spring of 1999, when we had Bruno for the last time. He was ill.

Learning from the Hubers was a special experience, but I needed my own tutor and Joyce Hopewell, a tutor and friend from the English Huber School came to the rescue. We had met on several occasions and she patiently guided me through the correspondence course to the completion of my Diploma in 1997. We were all happy that August in Adliswil, enjoying the reward for our efforts, the friendly company, wine, the beautiful garden of the Huber home, such a welcoming setting.

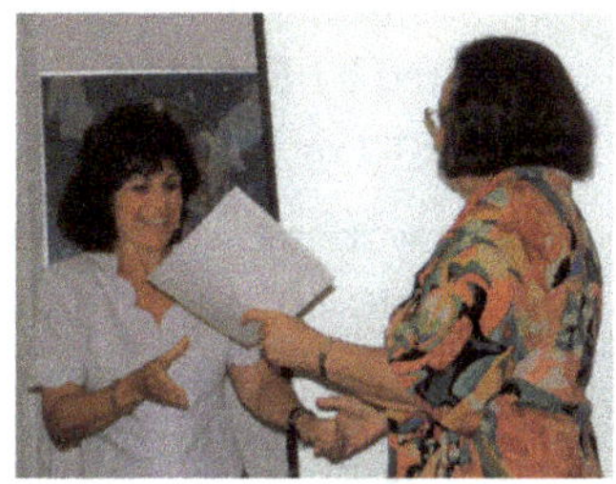

1997 Lola receives Diploma

At the VII World Congress in Luzern in 2000 Louise was still involved in the organising. She opened the Congress with her usual positive energy but everybody was thinking of Bruno, who had died the previous November. Richard Llewellyn and Joyce Hopewell were there: the Spanish School and the English School together, the growing network that was the continuity of the Hubers' great work. Bruno should have been in charge of the closing talk about "Models of transformation for the new millennium: the roles of Uranus, Neptune and Pluto." His presence was felt and deeply missed. A projection of Bruno's image on a huge screen reminded us of his vibrant personality and his work, and we all shared in the joy of having met him and enjoyed his charisma and his teachings.

When I returned to Adliswil a few years later there were sweet memories walking around the house and garden Bruno had loved so much. Gratitude is my main feeling associated with memories of Bruno and Louise Huber and their legacy. They planted many seeds that are sprouting all over the world.

Huber Software

The Spanish school stimulated the development of a new multi-lingual generation of software for the creation of Huber-style charts. Juan Saba from Argentina tells the story[169].

> After I discovered the work of Bruno and Louise Huber through the book *Astrological Psychosynthesis,* that I had bought during a trip to Spain in 1994, I began to study with the Spanish Huber School directed by Rosa Solé that same year. At the beginning lessons were delivered by regular mail, and then in 1996 we started with email.
>
> I was working with the advanced course work charts that I had been given but I had started in 1995 to do calculations with the program Astrocalc that kept the positions of the planets in a file. I started doing some simple routines in the programming language Quickbasic that helped me with the operations I had to do, and I even managed to draw the chart with my software.
>
> In 1997 in a lesson where I had to establish the strength of the personal planets to determine the strongest one, considering position in the chart, aspects, signs and houses, I designed the bar chart which is still in all my programs, and I sent it as part of my work to Rosa, who asked me how I had prepared it? I explained to her as above, and she asked if I could do something similar for all the tutors... so I started to design the program AstroCora.
>
> I distributed the program to the Spanish tutors and some students as a test. In Liérganes 1999 I presented my final course assignment work to Bruno & Louise Huber in Santander, Spain, and was awarded my Diploma. Afterwards I showed Bruno the work and gave him AstroCora, I remember installing it on his machine, the registration was sent later and in my records is dated Jul 1, 1999. He told me it was very good, and I remember he told me to keep it that way.
>
> After Bruno's positive comments I distributed many copies of AstroCora to students, and the Spanish version continues to this day.
>
> In 1999 Richard Llewellyn and Reynold Swallow contacted me, telling me that they knew about the program from Rosa and asking

169 Juan Saba, 'About how Huber Software began', personal contribution, May 2020.

Liérganes 1999
Juan Saba, Joan Solé, Bruno, Louise, Lola Cortina, Sylvia Sanchez

me if I could translate it into English, and that they would help me revise it. Thus was born the version that was used by APA students.

Also around 2000 API tutor Bruno Landolt contacted me by email from Switzerland. Bruno was distributor for another Huber software program (AstroVisa) that was based on the old DOS operating system. He had heard about my Windows program from a student in Israel who had purchased it from Reynold. Bruno offered to help me to develop a program for API, which we did, without any formal contract. I did the programming work and Bruno the German/Swiss distribution. Thus in 2002 the program Megastar was born[170].

In 2003, I was contacted by an APA student in Canada who was very happy with Astrocora and suggested I make a program for users in North America that would have both a traditional astrological chart capability and Huber chart capability. Thus the program Regulus was born in 2004.

In 2005 I presented Regulus with a stand in Norwac (Seattle), in 2006 in a conference at AFA and in 2008 at UAC where I gave also a lecture about the Huber Age Point.

A simplified version was produced in 2010 tailored to the requirements of the English Diploma Course – Regulus Student Edition.

As an aside, Juan reports that it was only after 20 years of collaboration that Juan Saba and Bruno Landolt realised that their mothers had been born on the same day!

---

170 MegaStar and the other software produced by Juan Saba are available on the website www.catharsoftware.com.

Expansion

2002-2008

Rosa continues the story of the Spanish school[171].

> Then came a period of expansion. From 2002 to 2008 Louise Huber came to Spain with her son Michael A. Huber to continue the training. These were intense years: Api-Ediciones – the publishing house which later published all the books by Bruno and Louise Huber in Spanish – was created by Joan Solé Girbau, the editor. Joan took over the task of organizing the courses that from that moment on were annual and often one-week long. The result was a very professional organization.
>
> Joan translated the study sets of face-to-face classes in Switzerland, all the articles written by Bruno Huber and published in *Astrolog* as well as the first volume of the Bruno's *Astro Glossarium*. The fruit of this gigantic work was the large attendance at the courses given by Louise and Michael, very special courses with a vitalizing and transforming energy in the sense that the group energy was cathartic and healing on a personal level.
>
> From this stage I fondly remember Louise for her adoration of Bruno's memory and her tenacity in preserving all the work done by both for so many years – the strength of Taurus which inspired great respect and also the sensitivity of Cancer, which stepped down to family level the concepts of the esoteric philosophy of Alice Bailey. Louise also confided her concerns about the future of API. Her Sun is in conjunction with my Venus in Taurus.

Louise, Adliswil, 2005

> Following this stage of expansion, several graduates from Spanish-speaking countries, e.g. Ana Quiroga in Chile, Juan Saba in Argentina, Martin Ochoa in Colombia... now have their own Huber centre where they teach their courses.

---

171 Rosa Solé, Op.Cit. Personal contribution.

Moving Online
2009-2020

Rosa's story continues[172].

For some years Michael Huber continued to come to Spain to teach annual courses on his 'planetology'[173], not always in line with the teachings of his parents. When Michael and then Louise had moved to Salzbergen, Germany in 2013 this was the end of the Hubers' direct connection with Spain.

Michael, Adliswil, 2005

There are currently several professionals and centres in Spain that impart Huber training. Api-Ediciones closed the publishing house in 2016 and all the books, seminars, articles... that had been translated from German into Spanish are open to the entire astrological community (free access) from its website[174]. Also, the first Spanish diplomate of API José Antonio Rodriguez[175], developed a free Huber software program[176].

The physical centre of the Spanish School in Barcelona closed in June 2019. The teachers now continue their work either through other centres or on a personal level. The online training continues to function with the same course that was translated from the English School, enriched by all the free material on the web.

At present

At 69 years old (2020) I am still fascinated by the practical utility, in the field of counselling, of the methodology developed by the

---

172 Rosa Solé, Op.Cit. Personal contribution.

173 Michael Huber's 'planetology', assembling the Huber charts into one, has never been documented, to the knowledge of the editors.

174 api-ediciones.com, section Library of Astrological Psychology.

175 Awarded by Bruno and Louise Huber at Exeter in 1992,

176 Free Huber software Astro-Nex, still available from astro-nex.net.

Hubers. And I fully subscribe to the use of cosmological symbolism as a path to personal freedom, a dialogue between our personality and the wisest part that guides us.

My commitment is that the symbolism and methodology of the Hubers' Astrological Psychology takes its place within the new professions, not as another predictive technique (with all due respect to those who use them) because we already are in the 21st century, but as a new and excellent tool at the disposal of individuals, of openness to their own essence, as stated at the end of the API Code of Ethics, self-responsibility and the freedom to be oneself.

11. The Huber/API Family

Those attending Huber events were almost without exception impressed by the openness, friendliness and humour of Bruno & Louise, and of their fellow attendees from across the world. In their own way, each was seeking to discover truths about themselves and the world, and Bruno & Louise provided the environment and the tools through which they would achieve that.

This family feeling was fostered by both of them, particularly Louise: "API is a kind of family in the wider sense. I have always cared like a mother for all the API family.[178]" It did indeed feel like one large extended family, with wise father Bruno and nurturing mother Louise at its heart.

In this chapter we present a selection of memories, stories and tributes to those involved and the spirit of those times – reflections from various members of that API family.

The API Centre in Adliswil

Joyce Hopewell reflects on her visits to the API Centre.

The two low-level wrought iron gates at the driveway of number 4, Obertilistrasse, Adlwisil, bear a sign announcing that this is the home of the Astrological Psychology Institute. The API logo, in bright orange, stands out against the sign's white background, while a pair of small stone lions sit, like sentinels, on top of the gateposts.

Built on a hillside in a residential area of the small town of Adliswil, this large house was where Bruno and Louise Huber lived and worked from 1983 until 2009. Prior to this, they lived in an apartment across the River Sihl on the other side of town, behind shops lining the main street. Richard Llewellyn stayed there when he was in discussion with the Hubers about setting up the English Huber School. When they moved to Adliswil, Richard recalls Bruno saying that the move happened

178 Bachmann, Op. Cit., Louise interview.

The API Centre, 1997

appropriately on a transit of Uranus. The house provided a permanent base as an educational institute offering study courses for groups of students and had both a consulting room and an office each for Bruno and Louise, with a large basement where *Astrolog* was produced.

Through the gates, past the garage to the right, is a paved patio area with benches and a low wall overlooking the steeply wooded hillside. Trees here provide shade in summer, making this a pleasant place for students to sit. The heavy wooden front door opens onto this patio.

The house, white with burgundy red shutters, is built on three floors, with a large hallway and a curved wooden staircase. The ground floor was the working area, the main seminar room being the focal point with other rooms leading off it; Louise's office to the right, the API office to the left. Bruno's consulting room on the right opened onto the hallway and was lined with glass-fronted cabinets filled with books and his collection of rocks and semi-precious gemstones. Across the hall was the small breakfast room and kitchen, Louise's domain, where she made sure the coffee machine was topped up, biscuits were laid out, and flasks of hot water were filled ready to supply break time drinks. Louise enlisted visitors or students to help get this ready; woe betide those who didn't get things organised in good time! The kitchen gave access to a larger dining area at the side of the house, called their winter garden.

Courses were held in the light and airy main seminar room, with three windows looking onto the garden. Pictures on the walls include some of Bruno's paintings, a print of galactic nebulae, and an enlarged photographic print of a painting by Nicholas Roerich, taken by Bruno

Seminar room, 2005

at the Roerich Museum in Moscow. Bookshelves contain a variety of astrological volumes while small golden ornaments of the Sun and the Moon hang on the walls.

The impressive marble fireplace is usually obscured by a free-standing screen used to project images of charts and teaching material. Tables and chairs would be arranged to face the table in front of the door to Louise's office. This table was often covered in a cloth bearing astrological glyphs. There was a brass bell of Indian design, which would be rung to attract attention when the session was about to begin. Bruno and Louise would sit here and teach, either singly or together, Bruno with his thermal coffee mug by his side.

The garden was a focal point during breaks. It was square, with a path and low wall around the perimeter. Trees provided screening from the road, there were flower borders, a rowan tree bearing clusters of red berries in late summer, and a wrought iron sculpture of an armillary sphere. The central lawn had, according to Louise, three significant energy points: Sun, Moon and Saturn points. Students would enjoy standing on the point associated with whichever ego planet they were working on or associating with. On the day of the Harmonic Convergence[179], Louise led the group I was part of in a meditation in the garden. We laid in a circle on the grass with the tops of our heads touching the Sun point. Louise, as always, was more mystic; Bruno, being more scientific, declined to join in.

---

179 Harmonic Convergence – the world's first synchronized global peace meditation, August 16-17, 1987, coinciding with an exceptional alignment of planets.

In the garden at Adliswil, 1991

At the end of a seminar, there would be a party in the garden. If diplomas had been awarded this was a good reason to celebrate. Bruno would fetch the barbecue from the garage and fire it up. Louise would have done the shopping for bratwurst, bread, salad and dessert. Students would be roped in to help bring bottles of red wine and sparkling water up from the cellar, and set up a long table with the food. From the garden there were views towards the surrounding hills, leading to Uetliberg, Zürich's mountain. Bruno often mentioned how much he liked this view. Along the ridge runs the Planetenweg, a designated walking path with a model and information on each of the planets laid out in comparative distances each planet is from the Sun. The planet positioned nearest to the house is appropriately – and perhaps synchronistically – Uranus.

In the corner of the garden, looking out on this view, is a brick-built summer house, with a small alabaster statue of the Venus de Milo on the corner shelf. Benches and chairs surround a circular table upon which stands a quirky ornamental green frog with a wide open mouth, which is used as an ash tray. Bruno smoked a lot; Louise was a social smoker, only lighting up on occasions like parties, or after a meal. After the bratwurst was eaten and the wine glasses had been refilled, people would gather in the summer house to talk and sing.

As darkness fell, the party would get lively as one person after another taught everyone a song from their own country. Louise thoroughly enjoyed these evenings as she loved company and was fun to be with, very different from when she was teaching and being serious. She especially seemed to like favourite old English songs, such as *Nellie Dean* and *My Bonnie lies over the Ocean*. It was several years before she realised that the words she'd been singing for this one were wrong; she'd thought it was *My Body lies over the Ocean*!

The Hubers' living and sleeping quarters were on the first floor. They retired here at end of a teaching day. The sitting room, with a large tropical fish tank, was above the seminar room. French windows opened onto a balcony, where Louise would sit and meditate early in the morning, wrapped in a shawl if it was cold. Her consulting room was on this floor, with a sofa bed could be converted into a guest room. The top floor could be used as a self-contained flat; here was Bruno's studio where he painted and experimented with the use of colour and shape.

Bruno's office was on the first floor. I was part of a small group of international teachers of astrological psychology invited here to learn more about how he was integrating the growing use of computers and the internet into their work. Plants sat on the windowsill and bookshelves lined the walls. Books were joined by a variety of ornaments – a brass candlestick, model cars, aeroplanes, lorries, trucks, a red London bus – many were mementoes of places they'd visited. A phrenology head, marked with the different brain functions, stood on a high shelf, and there were numerous coloured pens and pencils on his desk – very much a working desk – along with papers, books, magnifying glass and ashtray. A wall clock showed the signs of the Zodiac in place of numerals. Some of Bruno's paintings hung on the walls, along with another enlarged print of mountains by Nicholas Roerich, reminiscent of the shaping in Bruno's chart. The meeting over, Bruno and Louise insisted we join them for an aperitif before lunch – their favourite Campari. The meeting ended on a convivial note.

A group in Bruno's office, 1997

Bruno & Louise

We present here reflections, memories and tributes from some of the key members of the Huber/API family.

Bruno & Louise – Richard Llewellyn[180]

Bruno may have been the 'brains' behind the Huber School but without Louise it would never have blossomed in the way that it did. In her true Taurean way she was the solid foundation stone which enabled Bruno to do what he did for astrology, however difficult she sometimes found that role.

Louise may have been a tower of strength but her Cancer Moon made her emotionally sensitive not only to her own emotional needs but also to those of almost everybody with whom she came in contact through API. Though, in true Taurean fashion, if she was doubtful about someone when she first met them it wasn't always easy for her to get past that barrier. So what a wonderful thing it was to watch Louise's expression change from doubt to a sudden realisation that here was somebody who really knew what they were talking about, and that lovely smile would appear on her face and she would probably say 'Ahh, soo...!'

I have so many memories of times spent with Louise and Bruno sharing their wisdom, their knowledge and the life journey which they had travelled together. For me, Louise was so, so special and I loved her and Bruno dearly, and I believe that what they contributed, not only to my life but to the world of astrology and human evolution in particular will be seen to be yet one more important stepping stone on the path forward to a more enlightened humanity.

Louise, Richard, Bruno, Froebel, 1992

180 Richard Llewellyn, 'Remembering Louise Huber', *Conjunction* 65, May 2016, page 9.

The Gift of Bruno & Louise – Pam Tyler[181]

Bruno and Louise role modelled transparency as astrologers. From the beginning they were totally straightforward about their own horoscopes. Unlike many astrologers who 'hide' behind their birth data, Bruno and Louise routinely published their own horoscopes in books and used them as examples in lectures. They demonstrated an utterly fearless non paranoid attitude about sharing them.

But the purpose for doing so was never self-serving or self-aggrandizing. The point was never 'all about them' but rather a way of showing a healthy degree of detachment and vulnerability. It was also an oblique critique of power motivated astrologers who manipulated clients via secretive or seductive airs.

Bruno and Louise's mixture of candour and reticence was especially obvious when either one engaged students about their own horoscope. Their tone was always upbeat, constructive but never intrusive. The experience could be as much healing as it was edifying.

There are so many more questions I would ask Bruno and Louise if they were still alive. The House Chart never really made sense to me. I understood the rationale behind it but was never really comfortable applying it. I would probably also ask them to say more why they found "Trinity Cathedral" in Miami extraordinarily beautiful compared to the dark immense cathedrals of Europe which they avoided at all costs. Yes, Trinity Cathedral has exquisite light and glittering mosaics but my guess was there was more to the story.

The last time Bruno spoke to me I pressed him about Transits and Progressions. Did he really believe they were not important for astrological psychology? Bruno conceded that they could be helpful so long as they were subordinated to Age Progression, contextualized to the natal chart and never used as a predictive measure.

Bruno and Louise left indelible impressions but one in particular. Recalling again that first AFA Convention in Atlanta, their talk was in one of those massive hotel conference rooms with formidable but squeaky entry doors. Bruno was standing up front relaxed, casually dressed in his signature western bolo tie awaiting the signal to begin.

181 Pam Tyler, email to editors, May 2020.

Louise stood guard at the back door. Although garbed in a floral dress, her erect posture suggested a uniform. Walking in late would not have impressed her. But when Bruno started speaking this all changed. A broad smile crossed her face, she was beaming with pride. I do not recall ever seeing Bruno lecture without Louise front and centre or guarding the door. It was not always the case the other way around. Louise frequently spoke without Bruno side by side or in the background. But Louise did not mind. After all Bruno needed to rest because he stayed up every night as she told me "thinking, thinking, thinking". Louise was no minor figure in this partnership.

Yes, she was overtly protective of Bruno but full of her own gravitas. She wrote books, gave lectures, taught classes, counselled clients and probably bore the lion's share of administrative responsibility related to the World Congresses and assorted API activities.

What gift they both were to all of us.

The last time – Pam Tyler

The last time I saw them was in Miami around 1990. Bruno was quite enamoured by the tropical foliage, giant frogs, and colourful birds around my yard. He took lots of photographs. However, it was the mosaics at Trinity Cathedral that left him speechless. When Louise walked into the cathedral she exclaimed:

"PAAAAAAAMeLA dees eees a beeeeeeeuutiful church not like dee cold dark ones in Europe and England. Dees ees so full of 'light." But EES it dat way really? I mean dee people? Are dee people full of light too?"

Louise always asked the right question. They both did.

Salad – Rosa Solé

I remember Louise's endless advice and Bruno always being contrary with his sense of humour. "Bruno's salad" was always famous during the courses in Spain. Louise asked for salad for Bruno because it was healthy food and Bruno always refused to eat it because he didn't like salad!

Bruno & Louise – Joyce Hopewell

The large group of people who had gathered in the bar at Exeter University drew my attention because they were laughing and singing *The Happy Wanderer*, a popular song from the 1950s. Translated from the original German, its catchy chorus sounded like yodelling and was often heard on the radio in my childhood. Whatever was going on? UK astrological conferences, in my then limited experience, weren't especially "life and soul of the party" events. But in 1985, Bruno and Louise Huber had been invited to speak at the Astrological Association's annual conference. As more people drifted over to join them as they yodelled and sang this song, I looked on and wanted to know more.

I was still fairly new to astrology. I had successfully completed the Faculty of Astrological Studies' Foundation Course, had already embarked on their Diploma Course and this was my second conference as a budding astrologer. I'd never heard of the Hubers and was still building up a knowledge of the work of established UK astrologers and different approaches to the subject.

Realising I'd already missed Bruno's talk, I decided to go next morning to Louise's session on The North Node in your Chart. Hearing her speak was a life-changing experience as far as my astrological path and career was concerned. I was blown away by what she said and how she said it. Her slightly imperfect but totally understandable English conveyed a depth of knowledge and understanding of human psychology and the potential for personal and spiritual growth. I had to know more.

A few months later, in January 1986, after attending an introductory weekend run by Richard Llewellyn, I ditched the traditional Diploma Course I was studying in favour of the English Huber School's new Diploma Course in Astrological Psychology.

My first personal encounter with Bruno and Louise was in August 1987, when I went to the API Centre in Adliswil for a weekend seminar which included assessments by the Hubers for students of the English Huber School who had successfully completed the Diploma Course. The additional award of the Swiss Diploma by Bruno and Louise was the icing on the cake. I was meeting them face to face for the first time to present my chart and my understanding of astrological psychology, and hopefully to be awarded their Diploma.

Louise, Joyce, Bruno, Froebel, 1992

I remember my nerves at the prospect of standing up and talking about my own chart and life experiences to the group and to Bruno and Louise, but their sensitivity, kindness and understanding were always there. Bruno was encouraging, wanting to make me feel more at ease, and offered me his extendable pointer to use as I talked about my chart, displayed on the screen. Louise listened intently – I remember her eyes focussed on me – and she asked questions after my presentation. Speaking about my life experiences and relating these to my chart required being honest and open. I was one of the first English Huber School students to do this, but many more followed in subsequent seminars in Adliwsil, Achberg, London and Devon.

At the start of each seminar in Adliswil, Louise made everyone feel welcome in her home, beaming her wonderful smile, making sure students were settled in at the Kröne Hotel where she'd booked rooms, offering welcome drinks and refreshments. She was a good hostess, relaxed and friendly, only becoming more serious when teaching. With dark hair and eyes and an upright carriage, when sitting and standing, she had a powerful personal energy which she attributed to her First Ray personality.

Whereas Louise's voice was deep and strong, Bruno was more softly spoken. Louise spoke English with a noticeable German accent; Bruno's spoken English had a soft lilt, akin to his native Swiss German. He said that he'd begun learning English by watching American films, and his accent retained a slight twang. His English was excellent, and he could easily make jokes and puns. Both Bruno and Louise must have learned Italian whilst working in Florence, but the only experience I had of this was when speaking to Louise on the phone; she would always sign off with "ciao".

Bruno 1998

Bruno dressed casually, in a relaxed and stylish way, shirt sleeves often rolled back, bare feet in espadrilles. He liked leather belts, their buckles set with semi-precious stones, and wore a silver cuff bangle on his right wrist. Bruno never wore a conventional neck tie, preferring a bolo tie[182], of which he had several, with clasps set with gemstones, or in silver, or inset turquoise. His favoured and probably most treasured bolo was an enamelled reproduction, in colour, of his own chart, which had been presented to him by Swiss API students. In his latter years, when ill, he took to wearing a gold five-pointed star that had belonged to Roberto Assagioli.

API Jubilee 1998

Louise was always smart and well-dressed. She favoured dresses with matching jackets, sometimes skirts or trousers with an eye-catching top, usually in bright colours. Several of her preferred designs veered towards the ethnic and tie-dyed, and she always wore jewellery, typically necklaces of semi-precious stones and gemstone pendants. The gold bracelet on her right wrist was always there, as were her rings on both hands.

Louise was a good teacher in the seminar room and at home she was a good cook. Her Moon in Cancer shone through if she was preparing a meal for visitors. When it was ready she would ring the dinner gong in the hall, which meant come at once; she did not approve of late arrivals at the table! Food was important for Louise and her Taurean love of this was often seen. For lunch time breaks at seminars in Adliswil we would, as a group, often go to the nearby Blumenau restaurant, where Louise would have booked a table. Other Adliswil favourites were the Capri, an Italian pizza restaurant, and the Grüt Farm, specialising in chicken dishes. Bruno and Louise's favourite restaurant was in the Hotel Belvoir in nearby Rüschlikon. Overlooking Lake Zürich, this was where

182 A bolo tie is a type of necktie consisting of a piece of cord or braided leather with decorative metal tips and secured with an ornamental clasp or slide.

they liked to take visitors who were staying with them. The food was excellent. Bruno would always order his favourite dessert – a colonel – lemon sorbet served with a measure of vodka. The colonel was Bruno's signature dessert, and when a small group of us ate with Louise at the Belvoir sometime after his passing, we left a vacant chair for him at the table, and ordered a colonel to be placed there for the dessert course. After saluting Bruno, we each shared a small portion.

When teaching, Louise often referred to the books of Alice Bailey and often mentioned the Arcane School. She told students that she always had one of Bailey's blue-bound books by her bedside, and would read a short passage from it every night before going to sleep. On one occasion I was staying at the API house along with several other international representatives of API schools. Louise had invited us all to stay. It was a full house and she asked if Rosa Solé and I would share a room – and Louise's large double bed. As friends we were happy to do this, and delighted to see one of the blue books on her bedside table, just as described. [In Rosa's memory she can still hear Louise's words when she came down the next morning: "Have you had any special dreams"?]

There is no doubt that Louise was the practical, hands-on manager of API. She was the person who got things done. Bruno was an artist, experimenting with the use of colour, and a keen photographer. He was more concerned with creativity, ideas, research, and development of the Huber Method, leaving the practical organisation of the house and API to Louise. He kept different hours, staying up late into the night, thinking, writing, studying, researching. He was never around at breakfast time, maybe putting in an appearance for mid-morning coffee, but certainly for lunch.

Bruno was always interesting to talk with, and a good listener. Sometimes our conversations would be about astrology, when I was seeking clarification on a point used in the Huber Method. When I was preparing to take over the running of the English Huber School, Bruno asked how I felt about this, and where my Age Point was. I told him it was on the 8th house Low Point. He smiled and simply said "Perfect". Some time later I realised the significance of his question and my answer, when Louise spoke of the Low Point being a time when we are closer to the soul's purpose. Then it made sense.

1975

Bruno loved travel and he and Louise shared many trips abroad to speak at conferences or give seminars. They would stay on, hire a car and do their own road trip to see the sights. But when at home, they would take a separate annual holiday. Louise liked Davos in winter; Bruno headed for Provence in summer. He joked that every year he would vow to go somewhere different, yet he always found himself driving towards the south of France. On one occasion, when stopped at the border and asked for his passport, he proffered a laminated credit card sized version of his chart, telling the puzzled frontier guard that it could reveal far more about him than his passport, but he still had to produce the real thing!

Bruno and Louise came to the UK several times to give seminars and assess successful English Huber School graduates for the award of the Swiss Diploma. Residential workshops were held at Froebel College in Roehampton and at the Beacon Centre near Exeter. On one occasion, a piece of their luggage containing all their teaching material was lost and didn't arrive at Exeter airport with them. After many phone calls to the airport, the missing luggage was promised for the next day. I drove Bruno to the airport to collect it. Once it was safely retrieved, we were able to relax on the drive back, talking about places we'd visited. He was very good company and I treasure the experience of that very ordinary drive with an extraordinary person I was fortunate enough to know.

On two occasions, Bruno shared his experience of losing time whilst in Capolona (page 43). He had lost all track of time as he entered a trance-like state and had visions of the past and the future, and in particular, the way in which astrology and psychology could be combined. He spoke of seeing patterns, shapes and colours, from which emerged his use of coloured aspect lines and patterns denoting inner motivation. He only spoke of this to a few people, mainly those who were teaching and representing his work in different countries in the world. He also spoke more publicly about how he envisaged astrological psychology and the work of the Hubers developing beyond API Switzerland. His vision was that there would be "lots of little APIs" where students of this method would be teaching and passing it on to others. In many countries, this has become a reality.

When I began studying the Huber Method, I was enthusiastic, but at the same time sceptical in a healthy, open-minded way. I set aside much of the conventional and traditional astrology I knew, stayed open and kept testing out this new approach I was learning. I had doubts about the effectiveness and validity of Age Progression and Low Point planets when I learned about them, so used my own chart and life experience to experiment and apply the techniques to my chart and myself. To say I was blown away by the accuracy of Age Progression and the uncomfortable truths about myself I was confronted with by a specific Low Point planet are understatements. I was convinced. I never once looked back at the traditional astrological route which had led me to the Huber Method, and was quietly gratified when I heard Bruno say, in a teaching session:

> Don't think because 'Huber says this, or Huber says that' it means it's right. You have to test it out for yourself and see if it works. It's the only way to go.

Schnurri – Joyce Hopewell

Louise was not someone to cross; she had a lot of Taurean stubbornness, determination and a strong will. She once demonstrated her First Ray at work when their cat, Schnurri (Purry) was on the far side of the garden in Adliswil. Louise called to him, in German and in a powerful, commanding voice, "Schnurri, komm hier." Cats are not renowned for their obedience, but he stalked slowly across the lawn with eyes fixed on her and sat at her feet.

Bruno's Clicks Research – Barry Hopewell

I recall Bruno saying how, at age 19 with AP opposite Mercury, he researched the subject of 'clicks' between people's charts. He sat on steps in the centre of Zürich and observed passers-by, observing inwardly whether he felt a connection with the person. Then he asked for their birth data and checked whether the connection indicated in their and his charts corresponded with his own perception. I was slightly sceptical that the young Bruno might have found a great way to speak to a lot of pretty girls!

Bruno & Louise – Sue Cameron

In 1988, a year or so after I started studying with the English Huber School, I met Bruno & Louise for the first time. They had come to England for a week-long residential seminar, including diploma assessments, at Froebel College. It was an international gathering of around 50 people, all of whom had a common interest: to be with this charismatic couple and learn, at first hand, about their approach to astrological psychology.

On meeting Louise I remember thinking that she was an unbelievably strong woman, both mentally and physically – a hug from her was all-encompassing with no escape until she released you! She had a distinctive way of speaking, rolling her 'Rs' beautifully, as in Saturrrrrrn. The group meditations that she led were very special. During one of Louise's teaching sessions, I had the good fortune to have my chart interpreted by her. There was a focus on my Pluto conjunction to the North Node and, as I write this, my Age Point is in the middle of that conjunction. Louise reached deep into the heart of my chart and reinforced my belief in the value of Huber astrology, which continues to this day.

1993 Bruno at Elba
Photo: family

I first met up with Bruno as he was walking around the lake in the grounds. He was taking a rapid succession of photos of Canada geese, I learnt later that he had been a professional photographer. His natural ability to capture form and colour were apparent in his distinctive way of presenting a chart "that the senses could comprehend and from which everything important could be understood at a glance". Bruno had a powerful mind with the ability to convey complex ideas in a way that was easy to understand. His teaching sessions flowed from a depth of understanding that reflected years of painstaking research into the methods he had developed and their application in psychosynthetic counselling.

In the summer of the following year, I went to Adliswil to do my diploma assessment and became part of a global network of Huber astrologers. I attended the remarkable Seven Rays workshop in 1998, which has been a focus of interest for me ever since.

Bruno: Inspiration and Close Colleague – Wolfhard König[183]

I think you can only describe another person through the experiences you had with him. As in quantum physics the measurement influences what is being measured, only the changing effect can be measured. So in a relationship, I can just describe my changing subjective experience in it. So I'm trying to describe, in the only true way that I can, the quintessence of a thirty year old relationship between Bruno and myself.

When Bruno and Louise first came to Münich in 1970 I was employed in a yoga school, whose director was in the Arcane School, as was Louise. Bruno and Louise held an astrology course, that I attended despite some scepticism as a science student. Bruno not only allayed my concerns, but got to me such that by the end of that first evening I was afire with him and his ideas. That was typical Bruno – the serious, collected way of speaking, the careful weighing of statements, the quite scientific kind of thinking and especially the bridge to modern psychological astrology, that struck me with amazement and growing enthusiasm.

It quickly became apparent to me that here was not only an astrologer, but a well founded psychologist. Since I was at that time into psychology, I was impressed to hear someone from therapeutic practice. It was soon clear that Bruno had experience not only of just giving advice, but also with intensive therapeutic practice.

A significant factor leading to a relationship of over thirty years was the importance Bruno gave to an ethical approach. I had already read Anna Freud and Erich Neumann's essays on a new ethics in psychology, and here was Bruno speaking of his new ethical approach that was eventually codified in the 'API-code'.

This was at a time when psychology was still dominated by the behaviourist Skinner. Bruno's approach was clearly on the side of freedom and respect for the self, and for the self of others. That was his motto. It showed in his truthfulness and openness. He was never one to go behind people's backs; he would say things openly. Bruno could disagree openly and leave the other person's dignity intact.

His openness and resulting possibly sharp conflict could be difficult to experience, and sometimes we needed a 'cooling down period', but it did in the end hold the seed for a deeper relationship.

183 Wolfhard König, 'In Memoriam - Bruno', *Astrolog* 113, Dec 99, page 7.

During this early phase of our encounter there was much to learn from Bruno: not just astrology and psychology, also for example colour dialogue. No sooner had I heard about this new and revolutionary element for the first time (1972), I was again fired up. For ten years I worked with colour dialogue in Münich in groups and in individual sessions. From one session Bruno and I each had more than a dozen dramatic pictures from group dynamic processes, I recall our sitting together on the train back to Zürich, supervising the results.

Unforgettable were the days, and part nights, when we studied the therapeutic processes, gaining profound insights about the psyche of men and their stages of development. In these pictures were symbols of the phylogenetic development of peoples, especially its cultural development in the stages articulated by Jean Gebser [archaic, magic, mythical, mental, integral].

Once on the way home a customs officer wanted to know 'what the paintings were worth', to collect customs. Prolonged violent discussion concluded that they only had scientific value and we were allowed to continue undisturbed. As we went on our way, Bruno burst out laughing.

Our most intense encounter arose in the middle years. After the end of my psychology studies and psychoanalytic training, I was armed with the latest psychological and therapeutic research. It was Bruno who brought this into the API school, and later also API International. It was amazing how Bruno gained from my understanding of the findings from modern depth psychology, from the new research of the 60s and 70s. He showed that the teacher could also be in the role of learner.

The depth of our encounter grew as we found that we were both in the depths of our soul sceptical of the world in which we lived and the way things were going. Discussion began as I noticed that Bruno was removing cigarettes from a container. On the inside of the lid was inscribed in Bruno's handwriting "To get to the Source you go against the current." This led to a conversation in which I said to Bruno, somewhat provocatively, "You are a reincarnation of Giordano Bruno."

He just laughed, but seemed to like the thought. But for me it was the greatest compliment I could give, because Giordano Bruno was one of the central key figures in my thinking and my beliefs. Astrologically it was Bruno's Uranus square Saturn and my Uranus sextile Saturn. We spoke of this often.

In the seventies, Bruno's intransigence in discussing intellectual and psychological issues troubled me deeply, as I him. Two small scenes illustrate this. After a lecture by Bruno a participant stood up and began "Melanchthon once said...", but Bruno interrupted violently: "Above all I ask my own thoughts." On another occasion, when there was a controversial discussion about the new dynamic calculations, Bruno excitedly threatened the aroused audience: "Whoever simply uses my astrology without question is my enemy."

Often this irritated participants, thinking that this was an exaggerated reaction. You can see it this way if you want. For me, I always understood at such times just how much Bruno knew about the subject, and how he found and valued his own truth. And how much he distrusted traditional thinking. This was probably a crucial prerequisite to be able to put forward this new way, this new thinking in astrology.

Who in the seventies at API Diploma seminars would have said that Bruno was brusque? Well maybe he was sometimes, because the reputation of API was at stake. But Bruno was able to learn. In the course of time it came about that API people gained a reputation for reliable astrological advice, helped many people, demonstrating that the API diploma was a valuable professional qualification.

In the last phase of the API consultant training, mainly in Achberg, nearly every evening Bruno and I sat together. The topics had changed. The concern of people for peace was now in the foreground, with the wars in Iraq and Yugoslavia. And the equally depressing fact that the first great civilization of human beauty, the Sumerians, the source of astronomy, of literature (Gilgamesh) and of the creation of astrology, ended in genocide. And how many genocides have since then taken place, not least in 20th century Central Europe. And would there ever be a world without genocide and without wars...

Often we sat late into the night on the terrace at Achberg, looked towards the sky, to the stars. Once stood four people, Bruno and Louise, Peter Göbel and I, arm in arm on the Achberger terrace and looked up at Jupiter. Involuntarily I stretched the bow internally, from those Sumerian Priests, who looked up at the sky and discovered the secret of astrology, to those people who studied astrology in Achberg together and looked at the sky, and especially to this Bruno Huber.

Bruno: Wanderer between the worlds – Esther Dietz[184]

"I see the goal. I reach the goal and then I see another.[185]"

The wanderer between the worlds: this image comes to me when I think of Bruno. He was such an uncompromising, serious, realistic, clear thinker with far-seeing vision; his illuminated vision of the hidden thousands of years in the great cultures of antiquity; and his vision, together with Louise for a holistic, ethical, human freedom with astrology reaching far into the future. In between was the everyday life, the courses, the lectures, the research, the formulation of theories, the art...

I got to know Bruno, especially in many deep-rooted conversations we had late at night in Elba. There we sat for hours at a small table, he with his coffee, me with my glass of wine. For what was soon 15 years, our conversations revolved around the values of ancient cultures, their scriptures, their religions, their gods, their stargazing, their cults. Bruno was a discriminating expert on the ancient world and its astronomical and astrological discoveries, so was it a great pleasure to speak with him. I loved the ancient Greeks and their philosophy, art and literature. Our conversations had an incomparable, wide ranging and harmonious tone.

I always had a deep desire that Bruno's immense knowledge should not be lost. These great ideas would come together in the *Astro Glossarium*.

Bruno wasn't an 'easy' researcher, visionary and teacher. He was through and through a philanthropist, a friend of humanity in the truest sense of the word. He was in all his work committed to the individual human being, and to humanity. Spiritual freedom and self-determination were to him the highest good, the involvement of man in the one humanity and the cosmos a fact, which this freedom in no way diminished.

I remember his world space meditation, high above the sea on Elba, on the rock, in the middle of the Macchia, not far from the cemetery. Here stood man before the endless vastness of the cosmos and sought freedom, love and understanding of his own way on the earth.

The last time I saw Bruno we walked high over Zürich. He looked for a long time over the arch of the city, and spoke in a lively and impassioned way of his love for the city that had been his life, and the inner life path, from Sagittarius to Aquarius, that his Age Point was currently on.

---

184 Tributes to Bruno Huber, *Astrolog* 113, Dec 1999, page 5.
185 Alice Bailey's transpersonal seed thought for Sagittarius, Bruno's Sun Sign.

I think Bruno went this way consistently for a lifetime.

"Water of life am I, poured forth for thirsty man.[186]*"*

Bruno and Beauty – Lola Ferrer[187]

What most impressed me about Bruno was how Beauty – and by Beauty I mean that inborn ability to connect with what is harmonious and bring it to earth – had a natural expression in his person and everything he did, his artistic, creative side. I could feel his connection to delicacy and deep art in his Pisces Moon trine his Scorpio Venus. Not only did he have an understanding of transcendent harmony but he was able to make it accessible to others. I had been into astrology for quite a time, about a dozen years when I encountered the Huber Method and there was one thing that captivated me most and had me enthralled for ever... and it was Bruno's clear and artistic design of the horoscope, the stylized way in which the colour signs were drawn, the clear outline of planets, the colour lines that could geometrically reveal the innermost soul of the moment captured in the chart. And it all had meaning, the technical side of the chart fitted perfectly with the artistic and astrological significance of the design.

Until then I had always been searching for a satisfying chart style that responded to my need to find astrological beauty reflected in a practical and clear wheel. I had tried my own designs following the classical outlines but there was something missing. There were always too many crossings, little colour, confusion and dullness. And that was not the mirror of the living entity I was searching to see reflected in paper: a perfect piece of the cosmos arrested in time.

But Bruno's design had it all, it was not only a highly aesthetic piece of work, but responded to my deep need that the meaningful instrument a chart was should have a sort of transcendent beauty in it. His investigations led to so many breakthroughs. And he was an artist too. The Colour Dialogue and the Golden Mean seemed to have found their place in Bruno's design and astrological concepts, such as the Age Point, the Dynamic Energy Curve, the House Chart, in the dance of so many psychological elements expressed all in One.

---

186 Alice Bailey's transpersonal seed thought for the sign Aquarius.

187 Lola Ferrer, 'Remembering Bruno & Louise Huber', by email May 2020.

Bruno and the Dolphin – Rosa Solé[188]

Bruno was for me a teacher in the sense of learning to be oneself. He led me to commit to follow my life's path and helped me to grow by accepting and managing my own fears. Later, I graduated in psychology following his path. I fondly remember the dolphin in the garden at Adliswil, also on Bruno's bracelet. He told us it was related to the temple of Knossos. The image of the dolphin has always accompanied me when taking important decisions. Its predecessor is a mythological animal related to Montserrat, which was in past times an old sea (we live near there). I also remember feeling the energy of the stones of the Sun, Moon and Saturn in Adliswil's garden. Magical memories. The meeting with my own group of souls.

At the farewell of Bruno's last course in Spain (Liérganes, April 1999), he enjoyed as usual the food, wine and contact with the participants. It was an excellent course on Rays, and on coherence and genuineness. Bruno radiated a powerful, contagious humanity to enjoy the present from the heart. "Let flow the present without being involved in emotional reaction" was one of his last pieces of advice when I express my concern about his health.

Graphic impression of dolphin by Bruno Huber

188 Rosa Solé, input by email May 2020.

Bruno, always one step ahead – Mirjam Bertsch[189]

What an abundance of colourful memories I have of those times. For example, on Bruno's 50th birthday, he with Louise presented me with the very first API Diploma. The most intensive contacts with Bruno and Louise have changed and shaped my life – in my personal and professional worlds. I am infinitely grateful!

What would have become of me, without Bruno, the lovingly tolerant, wise helper? So much time wasted, before one awakens to meaningful life. I once complained during one of our night trips. "Don't be concerned", answered Bruno in his simple practical way, "you have all eternity at your disposal!"

Now is he gone before us to this eternity. Always one step ahead, maybe to continue research in the other dimension, to one day challenge us with his great love of people – always on to the next level.

Cute trip, dear Bruno, we'll stay connected to you !

Louise: formidable fun – Barry Hopewell[190]

Some have belittled the contribution of Louise, believing that Bruno was the real originator of astrological psychology. As with all such myths, there is an element of truth – in that Bruno drove the astrological/psychological research and developed the new ideas. However, Louise was the organisational driving force behind their teaching activities, and it was Louise who had the deeper esoteric understanding from her grounding in the Alice Bailey teachings. They were actually a team, and the enterprise would have foundered without either of them.

When I first met Louise in the mid 1990s, she was a formidable lady, brooking no nonsense but also with an enormous sense of humour. Attending her seminars was a joy and a privilege – she always made fun of her troubles with the English language, but always got her message across.

The fun extended to mealtimes. I have a clear image in my mind of Louise at Alicante in 1996, standing and demanding 'FOOD', when the service was rather slow. It was during that event that I took this

---

189 Mirjam Bertsch, 'Abdankungsfeier Bruno Huber', *Astrolog* 113, Dec99, page 2, final part.

190 Barry Hopewell, 'Remembering Louise Huber', *Conjunction* 65, page 10, edited.

photograph of Louise and Bruno saying 'cheers' with Campari, which she immediately jokingly demanded we never publish.

Alicante 1996

I have a second clear image of Louise following Bruno's funeral in 1999. Joyce and I had travelled to Adliswil with Richard Llewellyn and we arranged to eat with Louise in the evening at a favourite local restaurant. When we arrived, on time, Louise was already seated alone at the table, looking absolutely bereft – which was no doubt how she felt after losing her life partner.

The last time we saw Louise was at a seminar she held with Michael in Adliswil in 2005. Here, Louise was still that same elemental force, and this is as I remember her. It was a shock to hear reports of her 'decline' to a retirement home a few years later – difficult to believe that such a force was no longer powerful. But it was her time, and now the founders are gone. We owe Louise a huge debt of gratitude.

Louise: a revelation – Sue Lewis[191]

I first met Louise and Bruno Huber in 1985, at a one-day workshop where they introduced Astrological Psychology to a large number of London astrologers. The Hubers were a charming couple who presented their method with youthful enthusiasm. Although I was not then ready to embark on a second diploma in astrology that would involve rethinking much I had learned with the Faculty, I was sufficiently interested to purchase a copy of Louise's *Reflections & Meditations on the Signs of the Zodiac.* These meditations for each of the twelve Sun Signs when energy surges at Full Moon facilitate the ego's alignment with the soul, as expressed through a shift of consciousness from traditional to esoteric planetary rulership, converting Alice Bailey's *Esoteric Astrology* into practical exercises. The second and last time I met Louise was at Buckland Hall in the Brecon Beacons, in 2003, where – accompanied by her son Michael at the final workshop on "Transformations" she gave in the UK – with her booming voice, she steered a large gathering

191 Sue Lewis, 'Remembering Louise Huber', *Conjunction* 65, page 9.

through several transformational journeys. Thereafter, a small group of us were privileged to present ourselves and receive our Diplomas.

For me, Moon Node Astrology, in particular, was a complete revelation. In Part 2 Louise set out the esoteric connections, the doctrine of immortality, and the practical rules for interpretation. As she explained, at death 'the bodies (even the subtle ones) return to the materia prima', while 'the spirit, soul, or self, persists forever' (p. 138). When Louise slipped quietly away, on 13 January 2016, her Natal Age Point was approaching Pluto, while her Nodal Age Point was on her Taurean Sun, which also received a trine from transiting Pluto in Capricorn. This was a natural moment for letting go of the physical, emotional and mental bodies. By the time of her commitment to the forest of peace on 2 April, transiting Pluto was making a Search Triangle with natal Jupiter and Neptune, transiting Jupiter a trine to natal Sun/Mercury, transiting Neptune a trine to natal Pluto, and transiting Uranus an Eye/Ear through semi-sextiles to natal Sun/Mercury and Uranus. All these benevolent and thoughtful aspects graced the ritual release of her reincarnating spirit, wherever it is bound, while on Earth the lasting legacy of Louise and Bruno lives on.

Louise, with Love and Gratitude – Ghislaine Adams[192]

To Louise, with Love and Gratitude

• For your constant and continuous dedication to furthering astrological knowledge and the spiritual truths hidden within.

• For so generously sharing your insights and understandings with all of us, your students, through your many talks and writings and for allowing these to be recorded and translated.

• For introducing us through your Huber astrological method of chart interpretation to a clear path of psychological and spiritual growth and personal development

• And, personally, for the warmth and encouragement that you gave me when I did my API presentation at your home in Adliswil.

You will remain a beacon of light and inspiration for all of us who have been blessed to learn from and with you. Thank you.

192 Ghislaine Adams, 'Remembering Louise Huber', *Conjunction* 65, page 9.

Impressions of Louise Huber – Ana Quiroga[193]

It was September 2005, and I was in the Monasteries of Les Avellanes to attend seminars and present myself as a candidate for the API Diploma. Then I met Louise, with her tremendous booming voice. I also remember Angela Wilfart translating as best she could, because sometimes Louise herself corrected her, when very funny situations would occur. I really liked her, it seemed to me that she carried Bruno inside her, and to feel her and see her, was to listen to the explanations of the bases, of how exactly the method had arisen. But she was also herself, with that strong presence and the simplicity of everyday language to express herself.

When it was my turn to present myself to her, I felt somewhat nervous, my greatest fear was that in my giddiness I would not know how to show my work. I could think of nothing better than to start with a short poem, which of course Angela had difficulties translating and Louise didn't understand anything! She looked at me amused and puzzled perhaps, and gestured for me to continue. It was beautiful, a privilege to have presented myself to her, then 81 years old. An opportunity like that would be difficult to repeat.

Brotherhood
(Octavio Paz)
I am a man: little do I last
and the night is enormous.
But I look up:
the stars write.
Unknowing I understand:
I too am written,
and at this very moment
someone spells me out.

I feel very grateful to have been in front of one of the leaders of this method of Astrological Psychology, because even today when I lack a guide or a layout when preparing the courses that I teach, I resort to the old seminars that Louise and Bruno taught, and they make sense. I read frequently, and I seem to be in front of his great presence, because now I can better distinguish her voice from Bruno's. I hear her talking to me, she didn't call me Ana, she called me "Chile", because she couldn't believe that I came from the South of the World to find her, Louise.

Louise with Ana Quiroga

193 By email from Ana Quiroga, Chile, August 2020.

A granddaughter's perspective – Samantha Breno[194]

Michael's daughter Samantha reflects on her grandparents.

They were always very busy and my siblings and I mostly saw them during seminars. However they did invite us for nice formal dinners every once in a while and we always spent Christmas with them. When we heard the gong we knew it was time to eat. Louise enjoyed cooking, always the same meals on the same day. She spoke of the limited food choices they had after the war and was so grateful for what she had today.

We loved to play at the API house, there were so many places to discover. Sometimes we visited them on ski holidays in Davos, always in the same rented apartment. Louise loved to ski. Every day in Achberg when we were swimming she came down to the pool, jumped in head first and spent a little time with us out of her busy schedule. We were always impressed by how fit she was.

Bruno was more introverted and quiet. He always seemed like a really wise calm owl, funny writing this now because Louise was a big fan of owls, and collected owl figures. He seemed to always be thinking or philosophizing. Everything he said always seemed well thought through to me.

Together they had a calm, very understanding way of talking to each other. For me she was the organizer and he was the thinker, giving advice or helping to solve a problem. A great team! Unfortunately he died when I was still young so my memories are not as profound.

We noticed that Louise took a lot more interest in us as we got older. At age 17-19, I spent the night at API every Monday and she was still, at almost 80 years old, always working in her office, but took time to chat. She supported each of the four of us financially to learn English at language school, and never forgot our birthdays!

I loved lunches with her and Michael. There was always at least one sentence including something like "oh that's because your AC is in this house on that planet." I didn't exactly understand but it made sense and made me smile. Life seemed easier to understand with their astrological explanations for everything. She and Michael appeared to have their own secret language that I couldn't always follow.

Louise was always hoping that one of her four grandchildren would follow in her footsteps but unfortunately we all chose different paths. But maybe one day one of us will find the way back to it...

---

194 From Samantha Breno, Bruno & Louise's granddaughter, by email August 2020.

12. Legacy

2009 onward

A conclusion

These words appeared in the UK *Astrological Journal*, 2017[196].

> The Hubers have given the world their system of astrological psychology, or the Huber Method, which can be used by anyone, without great astrological knowledge, to help in their own psychological and spiritual development. This system has been proved in practice by many thousands of students and practitioners in many countries. It is a system complete in itself – Bruno and Louise Huber's gift to humanity.
>
> Many astrologers may wish to add the Huber approach as part of their astrologer's toolkit, along the lines indicated by Charles Harvey when commenting on the English Diploma Course: "If you are considering embarking upon professional training in psychologically oriented astrology this Course deserves serious consideration as part of your studies. However, the very nature of astrology demands that each student should in a sense adopt the Medieval model and obtain the widest range of viewpoints and approaches."[197] But care is needed; it's important not to mix systems up without being aware of what you are doing.
>
> Astrological psychology provides a valuable tool for use in counselling, and has attracted many psychologists and psychotherapists. From his wide experience Bruno reported that "What I do in two hours, a good therapist needs one or two years to get the same clarity of picture."[198] While few would reach such a level, many counsellors are able to quickly home in on their client's current problems.

196 Barry Hopewell, 'The Hubers and their Legacy', *Astrological Journal* 2017.
197 Charles Harvey, "The English Huber School", in Astrological Journal, 1985.
198 Bruno & Louise Huber, *Astrology and the Seven Rays*, HopeWell 2006.

> Sue Lewis has reviewed astrological psychology from an academic perspective, and summarises: "The roots of its method lie in the esoteric wisdom of ancient civilizations, to which modern methods of restoring equilibrium between cognitive and sensory learning have been applied. The astrologer's gaze extends over three principal charts for interpretation, one facilitating insight into the Akashic records of the past, and another mapping the collective environment of the present, as well as the central imprint of birth, the beginning of the journey, showing the way to psychosynthesis and transpersonal development, and using that most appropriate of symbolic systems, the language of the cosmos."[199]
>
> From my own perspective, as one perhaps more interested in human development, I find the comprehensive Huber Method a major contribution to understanding our individual place as part of the one universe. It represents a simplified and usable subset of astrology, incorporating a valuable and practical emphasis on raising the level of our psychology and spirituality.

Bruno's final message

At the end of the couple's last English seminar together in Devon, Bruno ended with these closing words, which we could see as his manifesto for the way forward[200].

> There is a need for a certain purity of that kind of astrology which we do, because it is so different in many aspects from what astrology is now. You have perceived that, for sure, by yourself in your own surroundings. The main word is psychology, that is we go at the psychology of the human being because I'm convinced of the fact that the human being is mainly psyche. Of course you have a physical body but we handle our body also from our psyche. By psyche I now mean feeling and mind.
>
> Therefore psychology is the way to deal with human beings if they are in trouble, even if they are in physical trouble, because there is mostly a psychological reason for that. They select some sort of trouble out of a psychological condition in them so we have to detect these, clear them and then the trouble will go away.

---

199 Sue Lewis, Op cit. *APWET*, p. 175.
200 Bruno & Louise Huber, *Astrology and the Seven Rays*, HopeWell, 2006.

That is also true for medical problems. They always have a psychological background and doctors already accept that if the person is in good humour while sick the healing is better. That's at least something already, the acceptance of psychosomatic function.

So this psychological approach to astrology is, in the way that we do it, absolutely new to this planet. Big words! But it's new to this planet. Look around, read books, any number of good books, good astrology books – it's new, it's different.

You know the best of astrologers, of whom we can say to our students "do read these books", like Liz Greene or Stephen Arroyo, are psychologically deep. However, from my perspective, they are astrologically back in the Middle Ages. They use the techniques of the past and it doesn't ever really fit. They sort of twist it like this and make it fit. But it doesn't work out because it's not consistent.

The system of definition and delineation mostly used in astrology is mediaeval in its mental structure. It doesn't have the knowledge about human beings that modern thinking has and that modern psychology brings us in a very differentiated way. There is no way in the old terminology of astrology, I've tried for years and years to correlate modern psychological thinking with the wordings of delineations of the old patterned astrology. No way – it doesn't function because similar terms in the two fields may mean different things and similar things may have such different names that you never come to the idea "that's that". It doesn't work.

So this, for the time being, is the only astrology that really correlates the two fields into one. That's why it has this name "astrological psychology". It's one thing, it's not astrology plus psychology. I think that it's important that you keep that in mind so you will be always there standing up for this progressive modern approach to astrology. And you will have to stand up some times.

If other astrologers come up to you and say "Why are you doing this? Why is it not seven years instead of six years for the age progression and why do you have Saturn as the mother – it's no good" and stuff like this. You will have to stand up and say that that's the truth if you watch carefully. If you put Saturn to be the father or something else and you don't watch, then it may fit your argument but it's not the truth psychologically – it's not.

So, you're up to something in the world going ahead with this kind of astrology or astrological psychology. It is a certain responsibility which you have from a point of view of ethics. Because astrology is being applied to people, to human beings, and human beings can suffer if they are misled by wrong advice.

You can do damage and that's no good, or would you say it's good to do damage? I think certain realisations coming from this kind of psychology may hurt the client, but that's momentary. Then the client always has two possibilities – shrink back from this process, forget it, that is not accept it, or work it through.

We can deliver more than just a remark. That is different from 'normal' astrology – they give you a remark, a statement about that planet there and that ruler over there etc. and no further psychological explanation – they just name it with some words. We can go through explanations of how things are constructed and how they came about, as every psychologist does, only we have the tool of the chart, a diagnostic tool that is very fast.

What I do in two hours, a good therapist needs one or two years to get the same clarity of picture. This is not a pompous utterance, it is sheer fact. It's practice. So don't make too much of a point in front of psychologists, they don't like that. They don't like the idea that it can be shortened down to two hours, especially not the psychiatrists.

But life is incredibly interesting living with this astrological psychology. It's interesting, and you will see that more and more you will attract more interesting people.

In the first instance all kinds of people may come because they hear "Aha! Tell me when my mother will die, I want to get the money!" Greed is one thing, wishful thinking is another thing. It's all been projected onto astrology and astrologers love to serve that. Many, too many, still do.

So, in the course of time you will select just by doing right, not by making propaganda in that sense, but doing right because those who have been with you go to other people and tell them. That's the best way to do it. Mouth propaganda we call it, word of mouth.

Now, one thing which I think is important. If you do something which is so important and responsible and professional (it is professional, your astrological education is of the most professional you can get in this world), then you should also try to keep track of developments.

You should go on learning more and more about it. You learn in two ways. You learn from sheer practice from the material that comes from the clients, you get more and more live material which can fill in your understanding of charts. This is a way of automatic research and one should be a researcher, in that sense at least. That is, ready to learn more about astrological psychology each time I deal with a person. That's one thing.

The other thing is to try to catch up with developments that have been found within our special field. New discoveries. They will come to you through the written word, seminars, meeting up in small groups,...

You should do something about growing further into this fantastic new field of thinking in order to go with the times because the times are changing very fast. People are changing very fast, conditions are changing very fast, problems are changing very fast. So get with it, keep going with it – I think it's important.

Current situation – 2020

In its German-speaking heartland in central Europe astrological psychology continues to be taught as a professional qualification, much as it was in the Hubers' day. A critical mass of students had been created, and the system became self perpetuating.

In the English-speaking world there was only briefly a critical mass to enable such a professional approach to work, basically while the inspiration from the Hubers themselves was still present and until the momentum so gained had run its course. The teachings and courses are now available in book form and many practitioners, consultants and tutors are there, supported by the web presence of the Astrological Psychology Association. A similar sort of situation applies in the Spanish-speaking world, where the teachings and teachers are available to all.

Astrological psychology is still very much alive. As people turn away from the materialism that has given rise to climate breakdown and the plague of covid-19, perhaps the time is coming for a resurgence of interest in growing towards our true spiritual potential. Astrological psychology is there as one of the paths to help people forward.

Final thought

We are indebted to Bruno & Louise Huber, who dedicated their lives and harnessed their complementary talents to this successful enterprise of bringing together astrology and psychology.

In Alice Bailey's terms, these remarkable individuals were true *World Servers*[201].

A new science of man?

Did Bruno & Louise achieve their 'New Science of Man', as presaged in their first book *Man and His World* in 1975? There are no randomised trials with controls that will prove this to you. We are in the realm of symbolic mind, rather than that of rational mind. The testimony of thousands shows that, in the hands of an intuitive counsellor, or of an alert self-driven individual, the mandala of the Huber birth chart, reflecting the energies of the whole at time of birth, can reveal valuable information to help the psychological and spiritual growth of the person.

Piercing the eggshell?

Does astrological psychology provide a practical process enabling the psychological-spiritual growth of the practitioner or client? The evidence of personal testimony, such as those in this book, suggests that in the right hands this is indeed the case, that it can help to *pierce the eggshell* of the crystallised ego towards a more spiritual way of life.

In the spirit of Bruno Huber, you will only know the answer to these questions for real if you try it out for yourself!

201 See e.g. Alice Bailey, *Esoteric Psychology II*, p. 636, 'New Group of World Servers'.

Key Dates

The Hubers and API

1924 10th May, 03:15, Bamberg. Birth of Louise Huber (née Böck).
1930 29th November, 12:55, Zürich. Birth of Bruno Huber.
1952 Bruno meets Louise R.
1953 21st March, Zürich. Bruno & Louise marry.
1955 9th August, 17:17, Zürich. Birth of Michael Huber.
1956 Summer. Bruno & Louise go to Geneva.
1958 Spring. Bruno visits Florence.
1959 February. Bruno & Louise move to Florence to work with Assagioli.
1962 New year. Return to Zürich.
1964 Louise offers written horoscopes.
1968 12th March, 20:08, Zürich. Formation of API.
1970 Wolfhard König encounters Bruno.
1972 First Achberg summer school.
1975 First Huber book published *Man and His World.*
1977 Start of Elba and Morschach seminars.
1978 Bruno's first talk at AFA Conference.
1981 16th April, 19:00, Zürich. First World Astrology Conference.
1981 20th April. First Issue of *Astrolog*.
1983 Adliswil. Purchase of API House in Obertilistrasse.
1989 6th May, 16:05. Founding of API International.
1991 Bruno's heart attack.
1996 API on the internet.
1999 3rd November, Zürich. Bruno Huber died.
2001 API management team Louise, Michael, Wolfhard, Ruth S.
2002 Publication of *The Planets* completes the astrological psychology set.
2008 12th March. API 40th anniversary.
2009 *Astrolog* transfers to API International; new operation in Germany.
2009 28th February, 10:00, Zürich. New constitution for API International.
2009 31st March, Zürich. API Institute closed.
2009 22nd August, 15:18, Zürich, API International renamed Internationaler Fachverband für Astrologische Pychologie (IFAP).
2011 Adliswil. API House sold. Michael moves to Salzbergen.
2013 Salzbergen. Louise moves there.
2016 13th January, 12:45, Salzbergen. Louise Huber died.

English Huber School

1925 14th August, 06:19, Sidcup, England. Birth of Richard Llewellyn.
1945 19th September, 02:30, Tadcaster, England. Birth of Joyce Hopewell.
1948 19th November, 17:32, Ankara, Turkey. Birth of Pamela Tyler.
1981 Richard Llewellyn meets Pam Tyler.
1982 Richard goes to Sarnen seminar to work with Bruno & Louise Huber.
1983 8th June, 12:30, London. English Huber School / API (UK) created.
1984 First student enrolled. Bruno & Louise give seminar in Exeter.
1987 August. First API Diploma seminar in Adliswil for English students.
1988 First Froebel College, London, seminar in April with Bruno & Louise.
1989 October. First *Face to Face* workshop, Natural Health Centre, Totnes.
1990 April. API (UK) students attend seminar in Achberg, Germany, with Bruno & Louise; Dip. API awards given.
1991 Joyce Hopewell takes over as API(UK) Principal; Richard is Principal Emeritus.
1993 First of annual *Face to Face* residential workshops at The Beacon Centre, Exeter.
1995 Bruno & Louise give first seminar at The Beacon Centre.
1996 Easter. Bruno & Louise give first joint seminar in Alicante for Spanish and English students.
1998 Bruno & Louise give 7 Rays seminar at The Beacon Centre – their last together in England.
1999 Last *Face to Face* at The Beacon Centre.
2000 First *Face to Face* at Buckland Hall in the Brecon Beacons, Wales.
2001 API (UK) 18th Birthday; Wolfhard König seminar.
2003 Louise & Michael give last UK Huber seminar at Buckland Hall.
2003 September. API (UK) becomes Astrological Psychology Association. Joyce stays as Principal, and Richard as Principal Emeritus.
2004 Publication of *The Cosmic Egg Timer* by Joyce and Richard; first introduction to Huber Method, in English; new publisher HopeWell.
2005 Adliswil. Louise & Michael give last English-language Huber semiinar.
2006 Last *Face to Face* at Buckland Hall.
2007 *Face to Face* held in separate venues. First API (UK) Diploma's awarded.
2008 With *Transformation*, full range of Huber books now available in English.
2008 APA becomes Scottish limited company. Richard retires.
2017 Diploma and Foundation Courses published.
2019 December. Last EHS Diploma Course completions.

Spanish Huber School

1931 24th January, 11:58, Schwedt, Germany. Birth of Angela Wilfart.
1951 5th April, 16:17, Manresa, Spain. Birth of Rosa Solé Gubianes.
1977 Angela Wilfart meets Hubers at Achberg.
1985 Rosa Solé meets Richard Llewellyn.
1986 Rosa inspired by Hubers at Sarnen.
1987 Rosa enrols with English school.
1990 Rosa Solé meets with Wilfart and Llewellyn at World Congress, Luzern.
1990 15th April, 13:40, Luzern, Switzerland, Spanish Huber School founded.
1992 First Spanish Diplomate of API.
1993 First seminar by Bruno & Louise in Spain, Montbui.
1996 Easter. Bruno & Louise give first joint seminar in Alicante for Spanish and English students.
1999 Last seminar by Bruno & Louise together in Spain, Liérganes.
1999 Bruno approves Juan Saba's AstroCora.
2002 Joan Solé begins translation of Huber books, via API Ediciones, and articles, takes on API courses.
2002 Regular visits by Louise and Michael begin.
2002 MegaStar released by Juan Saba, in collaboration with Bruno Landolt.
2009 Michael Huber continues Spanish workshops on his own.
2013 End of direct link with Hubers.
2016 API Ediciones publishing house closed; all books and materials available free online.
2019 Barcelona centre closes down. Individual teachers and online courses carry on.

Bibliography

Books

Assagioli, Roberto, *Psychosynthesis: A Manual of Principles and Techniques*, first pub. 1965.

Bailey, Alice, *A Treatise on White Magic*, Lucis Press, 1934, p. 439.

—*Esoteric Astrology*. Lucis Trust, 1951.

—*Esoteric Psychology I*, Lucis Trust, 1936.

—*Esoteric Psychology II*, Lucis Trust, 1942.

—*The Unfinished Autobiography*, Lucis Trust, 1951.

Campion, Nick, *A History of Western Astrology II*, Continuum, 2009.

Grove, John, *Dreams and Astrological Psychology*, HopeWell 2014.

— *Life Passages: When Age Point Aspects and Dreams Coincide*, HopeWell 2017.

Fankhauser, Alfred, *Horoskopie,* Orell Füssli, Zürich, 1939.

Hakl, Hans Thomas, *Eranos: An Alternative Intellectual History of the Twentieth Century*, McGill UP, 2013.

Hopewell, Barry, ed, *Astrolog I; Life and Meaning*, HopeWell 2007.

—*Astrolog II: Family, Relationships and Health*, HopeWell 2009.

—*Astrological Psychology: The Huber Method*, HopeWell 2017.

—*Foundation Astrology*, ebook published by Astrological Psychology Association and available on its website.

Hopewell, Joyce *Aspect Patterns in Colour*, HopeWell, 2010.

—*The Living Birth Chart*, HopeWell, 2008 (bw), 2019 (colour).

—*Using Age Progression*, HopeWell, 2013.

Hopewell, Joyce & Llewellyn, Richard, *The Cosmic Egg Timer: Introducing Astrological Psychology*, HopeWell, 2018, first pub. 2004.

Huber, Bruno, *Astrological Psychosynthesis: Astrology as a Pathway to Growth*, 3rd English edn HopeWell 2006. First published in German in 3 volumes API-Verlag 1981-84.

—*Astro Glossarium I*, API-Verlag, 1995 (German).

Huber, Bruno and Louise, *The Astrological Houses: A Psychological View of Ourselves and Our World*, trans. by Haloli Richter, 3rd rev edn, HopeWell, 2011. First published in German API-Verlag 1975 as *Man and his World.*

—*Astrology and the Seven Rays: Interpreting the Rays through the Natal Chart*, transcribed from workshop at Beacon Centre, Exeter (1998), with additions, tr. Heather Ross, HopeWell, 2006.

—*LifeClock: The Huber Method of Timing in the Horoscope*, tr. Haloli Q. Richter, Transcript, and Agnes Shellens 3rd edn revd HopeWell 2006. First published in German API-Verlag in 2 volumes 1980, 1983.

—*Moon-Node Astrology*, tr. Transcript, Weiser, 1995; repr. HopeWell, 2005. First published in German API-Verlag 1991.

—*The Planets and their Psychological Meaning: Capabilities and Tools of the Personality*, tr. Heather Ross, HopeWell, 2006. First published in German API-Verlag 2002.

—*Transformation: Astrology as a Spiritual Path*, trans. by Heather Ross, HopeWell, 2008. First published in German API-Verlag 1996, extended version of *Life Clock III* (1985).

Huber, Bruno, Louise and Michael Alexander, *Aspect Pattern Astrology: A New Holistic Horoscope Interpretation Method*, trans. by Heather Ross, 2nd edn HopeWell, 2019. First published in German API-Verlag 1999.

Huber, Louise, *Reflections and Meditations on the Signs of the Zodiac*, tr. Moray Patterson, American Federation of Astrologers, 1984. First published in German AP-Verlag 1981.

Leo, Alan, *The Art of Synthesis*, first pub. 1912.

Lewis, Sue, *Astrological Psychology, Western Esotericism and the Transpersonal*, HopeWell 2015.

Parfitt, Will, *Psychosynthesis: The Elements and Beyond*, PS Avalon, 2015.

Rudhyar, Dane, *The Astrology of Personality*, Aurora 1991, first pub 1936 by Lucis Trust.

Articles

Most of these sources are from the magazine *Astrolog* (German) or *Conjunction* (English) or various astrology magazines.

Adams, Ghislaine, 'Remembering Louise Huber', *Conjunction* 65, May 2016, page 9.

Bachmann, Verena 'Interview with Louise Huber', *Astrologie Heute* 2003, tr Joan Solé into Spanish, then Sue Lewis into English, *Conjunction* 65, May 2016, page 13 on.

—'Interview with Bruno Huber', *Astrologie Heute 82*, Dec 1999, tr Joan Solé into Spanish, then Sue Lewis into English. Unpublished in English.

Bertsch Mirjam, 'Abdankungsfeier Bruno Huber', Astrolog 113, Dec 1999, page 2.

Dietz, Esther, 'Tribute to Bruno Huber', *Astrolog* 113, Dec 1999, page 5.

Ferrer, Lola, 'Baby Huber School comes of age', *Spanish Huber School bulletin* 60, Apr 2008.

Harvey, Charles 'The English Huber School', *Astrological Journal*, 1985.

Hopewell, Barry, 'The Hubers and their Legacy', *Astrological Journal*, 2017.

—'Remembering Louise Huber', *Conjunction* 65, May 2016, page 10.

Huber, Bruno, *When Someone Makes a Journey*, Bruno Huber. First published in German in *Astrolog* Issues 41,42,44,45 in 1987/88, and later in English in APA Booklet *The Development of Astrological Psychology*, 2017. Translated by Agnes Shellens.

—'Software', *Astrolog* 69, August 1992, page 10.

Huber, Louise, *The Development of an Astrologer – 36 years of API*, Louise Huber. First published in *Astrolog* Issue 139 in 2004. Published in English as APA booklet *The Development of Astrological Psychology*, 2017. Tr. Heather Ross.

—'API Formation Chart', *Astrolog* 231, Oct 2019, pages 13-15.

—'Der Werdegang des API', *Astrolog* 103, Apr 1998, page 6.

—'Wie es begann: Die ersten Nummern vom Astrolog', *Astrolog* 166, Nov 2008, page 8.

Huber, Louise & Landolt, Bruno, 'Die Erfolgsgeschichte des API', *Astrolog* 210, Apr 2016.

König, Wolfhard 'Bruno Huber, Psychologist and Astrologer', *Conjunction Digest III*, page 57.

—'Brief des Präsidenten', *Astrolog* 184, Dec 2011, page 34.

—'Der Astrolog', *Astrolog* 166, Nov 2008, page 16.

—'Bruno Huber, Astro Glossarium I', *Conjunction Digest III*, page 57, 58.

—'In Memoriam – Bruno', *Astrolog* 113, Dec 1999, page 7.

—'20 Jahre – API International', *Astrolog* 162, Mar 2008, page 2.

Landolt, Bruno, 'Astrologiesoftware, Computer und Drucker: Interview mit Bruno Landolt', *Astrolog* 129, Aug 2002, page 25.

—'Rückblick auf eine Erfolgsgeschichte', *Astrolog* 200, Aug 2014, page 22.

—'Zum 20. Todestag von Bruno Huber: Ein Rückblick auf sein Lebenswerk', *Astrolog* 231, Oct 2019.

Lewis, Sue, 'Remembering Louise Huber', *Conjunction* 65, May 2016, page 9.

Llewellyn, Richard, 'How the English Huber School Came Into Being,' *Conjunction* 58, Jul 2013, page 24.

—'Remembering Louise Huber', *Conjunction* 65, May 2016, page 9.

Meyer, Elsbeth, 'Netzwerk Astrologische Psychologie', *Astrolog* 207, Nov 2017.

Personal Contributions

Pam Tyler, Joyce Hopewell, Richard Llewellyn, Sue Cameron, Rosa Solé Gubianes, Lola Ferrer, Angela Wilfart, Juan Saba, Ana Quiroga, Harald Zittlau, Bruno Landolt, Elke Gut, Wolfhard König, Samantha Breno, Michael Huber (via Samantha).

Websites (www.)

English	
astrologicalpsychology.org	Astrological Psychology Association and HopeWell publisher
Spanish	
escuelahuber.org	Spanish School
api-ediciones.com	API Ediciones publisher
German	
i-fap.org	IFAP
astrolog-magazin.com	Astrolog
fernstudium-ap.org	Distance learning
Multilingual	
catharastrologysoftware.com	Software
astro.com	Charts and data

Index

www.ingramcontent.com/pod-product-compliance
Lightning Source LLC
Chambersburg PA
CBHW070916270326
41927CB00011B/2601

* 9 7 8 0 9 9 5 6 7 3 6 5 6 *